Nipped in the Ice

See page 172.

ARCTIC HEROES:

FACTS AND INCIDENTS

OF

ARCTIC EXPLORATIONS

FROM THE EARLIEST VOYAGES TO THE DISCOVERY OF THE FATE OF SIR JOHN FRANKLIN, EMBRACING SKETCHES OF COMMERCIAL AND RELIGIOUS RESULTS.

By REV. Z. A. MUDGE,

AUTHOR OF "VIEWS FROM PLYMOUTH ROCK," "WITCH HILL," "FOOT-PRINTS OF ROGER WILLIAMS," ETC.

FOUR ILLUSTRATIONS.

NEW YORK:
NELSON & PHILLIPS.
CINCINNATI: HITCHCOCK & WALDEN.
SUNDAY-SCHOOL DEPARTMENT.

PREFACE.

WE have endeavored in this volume to give the principal facts in the wonderful history of arctic exploration, down to the discovery of the fate of Sir John Franklin. We have not included, however, the Grinnell Expedition of 1853–5, sent out under Dr. Kane, which, though seeking Franklin, did not embody in its results any facts concerning him, but is yet so remarkable in its achievements, so full of thrilling incidents, and so rich in information, that we have reserved our sketches of it for another volume, which will embrace all the late arctic voyages.

In the arctic history here presented we have given the results of a wide range of study in this class of literature, including both that published in this country and in England.

In the orthography of words belonging to the extreme northern regions we have used the simplest form, supported by good literary authority, following mainly that of Professor Dall, of the Smithsonian Institution, in his standard work on Alaska. Thus, we have Esquimo, used in a collective and individual sense, Kamchatka, Bering, etc.; words more grateful to the eye, more easily written, and more readily spoken, than in their old forms.

Though mainly secular in character, our book will yet be found, we are persuaded, decidedly healthy in moral tone, and, in some of its chapters, of marked religious interest. It has been written for our young people, and from this stand-point the author wishes it to be judged.

Z. A. M.

CONTENTS.

Illustrations.

ARCTIC HEROES.

CHAPTER I.

NORTHMEN NAVIGATORS.

OUR readers need not shiver at the thought of a voyage into the regions of cold and ice. They will, of course, not wear their summer garments, but go clothed in the warmest furs; a material made by God for arctic wear, the equal of which for this climate no woolen factory would think of producing. They must go with a resolute spirit, too; for no timid, fireside dreamers, loving yellow-covered literature, the last dime novel, or sickly story books, need engage to accompany us. Should they wish to do so they must first throw all such trash into the fire, and agree to stand erect, facing the North Pole with unflinching bravery. To those who will do this, whether manly boys or womanly girls, we promise no small stores of useful knowledge, no little interest from thrilling adventures, and sometimes positive amusement from laughable incidents.

Do you ask where we are to go? Take a map of the Arctic Ocean. See where Spitzbergen projects toward the North Pole on one side, and, not far from it, where Greenland advances—we do not know how far—and where Nova Zembla and the Siberian Islands stand as sentinels at a very respectable distance. No part of the continents of Asia or America claims to extend as far as we propose to go. It is into what is marked as an ocean, spotted by these small portions of land, that we intend to sail, not neglecting, however, to make ourselves acquainted with the regions of cold lying a little further south.

What is called the Arctic Ocean is of vast extent. Its shore-line circle is many thousands of miles. Its area four and a half millions of square miles. It has a beauty and grandeur of its own. We shall not stop here to describe them, but will only say that its sky, at times, flashes with a light marvelous in its variety of form and color; its waters float icy islands wrought into magic forms, and its cold, thin atmosphere is fanned by wings of birds so many in number that we could no more count them than we could count the leaves in the forests of the sunny South. These we will show our readers in due time, if they do not leave our company.

We shall certainly introduce them to some of the bravest and best of men, and show them a peculiar people who live in a land of perpetual cold.

Who were the first visitors of the arctic regions? We cannot answer that question with certainty, but we know who were voyagers there many hundred years ago. A bold navigator from Norway, by the name of Other, sailed in A. D. 890 round the northern extremity of Iceland. He was the first to cross the arctic circle. This was a great voyage for a time when a ship was not as good as our shore-trading vessels; but he made no discovery. Some years afterward an Icelander, named Gunbiorn was driven off the coast of his country in a storm. Away his little bark scud before the wind, until it came in sight of a high rocky coast of an extended land. The storm had subsided, the wind changed, and so he steered for Iceland without going ashore. He reported his discovery, but nobody cared to try the stormy voyage, and for nearly a hundred years nothing more was known of it. In 982 a fierce Iceland chief became too turbulent to be esteemed by his king a safe subject, and was banished for a term of years. Being as bold as he was wicked, he wisely resolved to spend the time upon the ocean in search of unknown lands. It may be that he had heard of Gunbiorn's story. At any rate, he sailed away to the west, and came to the same great land. He stayed there with his ship's crew three years, learning all he could of its extent and character. He then returned and persuaded a colony to go to this land of promise.

This chief's name was Eric, known as Red Eric. He seems to have been a speculator in new lands —perhaps he formed a stock company; and, to make his speculation succeed, he called the new continent *Greenland.* Those whom he persuaded to go were much *greener*, we think, than the land. But good came out of his project.

Not long after the settlement was made, a son of one of the colonists, wishing to join his father, started in a ship for Greenland. He sailed a long, long time, driven by contrary winds and drifted by strong currents. At last he came in sight of land. He looked carefully toward the shore as he coasted at a safe distance. He came finally to the conclusion that this *was* a green land, and, as he had learned before leaving Iceland that Eric's Greenland was perpetually white with snow and ice, he decided that he had sailed out of his way. He steered to the north and saw other lands. These are now believed to have been Nantucket, off the coast of Massachusetts, Newfoundland, and Labrador. He reached Greenland all right in 987. He had not landed in any of these newly discovered countries.

Ships sailed in those days, it is said, four miles an hour in good weather, so that a hundred miles a day was good speed. Eric's long voyage must have made his sailors, if not seasick, very sick of the sea.

But Eric himself was neither. Thirteen years later, in the year 1000, he sailed through the same waters. He landed on Rhode Island, and, having examined the vicinity, made his winter-quarters at the mouth of what is now known as Taunton River. Here a woman of his company gave birth to a child, whom they named Snorre Thorfinnson. Little Snorre was, so far as we know, the first

American born of European parents. He called the country Vineland, because he thought it abounded in vines.

The spot where he made his winter-quarters, the birthplace of Snorre, is not far from Plymouth Rock, and was within the range of the excursions of the Mayflower pilgrims. It may be that Eric visited the shores of Plymouth harbor during the winter. In the spring he sailed away to Greenland.

These voyages were made nearly five hundred years before Columbus discovered America! So, after all, that great man only revived knowledge which the world had forgotten. But it does not rob him of his laurels. No printing-press had perpetuated the knowledge, and men were as ignorant of our great land in the fifteenth century as they were in the eighth.

After Eric's voyages occasional ships might have been seen in American waters up to the year 1347; but no colonies were formed.

These facts are obtained from the "Icelandic Annals"—old records of Iceland—which careful investigators of history have of late years examined very critically. A learned English writer says of them: "The authenticity of the Icelandic manuscripts seems to be fully established:"* and a recent American writer says of them: "These narratives are plain, straightforward, business-like accounts of actual voyages made by the Northmen,

* "The Polar Regions." By Sir John Richardson, LL.D. P. 30. Edinburgh. 1861.

in the tenth and eleventh centuries, to Greenland, Newfoundland, Nova Scotia, and the coast of Massachusetts and Rhode Island. Within the whole range of literature, of discoveries and adventures, no volumes can be found which have more abundant internal evidence of authenticity."*

The colony of Northmen in South Greenland became somewhat important in spite of its cold, its never-melting snow, and its distance from the civilized world. These old annals, which describe the voyages into the arctic regions, refer to the whales and seals, some of which were taken. An account of the way they caught the whales in those early days would be curious.

The Roman Church sent to the colony priests as early as the last of the tenth century. We have an account of the demand by the Pope of his "pence" from these colonists. It was called "*Peter's* pence," but we never could see what the good apostle had to do with it, nor do we believe these Northmen could; but they paid the demand with walrus tusks.

It is a singular fact of history that this colony became extinct nearly a hundred years before Columbus discovered the New World, and its memory was at the time well-nigh lost to mankind. "The Black Death," as it was called, which clothed other portions of the world in mourning, is held accountable in part for its decay; war,

* "Ancient America." By John D. Baldwin. New York: Harper & Brothers. 1872.

Death's ever ready helper, had its share in the work, and, it is surmised, the savage Esquimo added the finishing stroke. The reader will hesitate to charge this crime upon these people when he has made their intimate acquaintance.

Columbus' successful voyage opened a new era in the history of explorations. It began from that time to be carried on, not as by the Northmen, by reckless men on their own responsibility, but by Governments, and well-organized companies, through able, intelligent, and responsible navigators. John Cabot was such a navigator, and so was his son, Sebastian. They were Venetians, but lived in Bristol, England, and were sent out by the king and merchants of that country. In 1497 father and son landed on the coast of Labrador, and then voyaged along the coast of America to Virginia. The next year the son made a northern voyage alone; afterward he made an attempt to find the north-west passage into the Asiatic seas—the first, it is said, of the many attempts which have occasioned most of the history of which we are writing. He expected to sail quickly to the land where "spices do grow," but instead he found, as he declares, "such greate heapes of ise which I durst passe no further." All was cold and dreary—no balmy breezes nor fragrant odors. Even the people disgusted him, being "like brute beasts in their behavior, dressed in beasts' skins and eating raw flesh." Yet he meanly kidnapped three of them to carry home as specimens! How would he have liked it if the Esquimo had stolen *him?* Thus, with his nose turned up at the country and its people, yet keeping three of them unlawfully and unmercifully under his nose, he sailed away South, and discovered Florida. The natives of this country would not have been as amiable as were their northern brethren had an attempt been made to select specimens from their number!

In 1500 Gaspar Cortereal, a gentleman brought up in the court of the King of Portugal—a man of learning and ability—sailed into the arctic seas in command of many ships, made important discoveries for hundreds of miles above Labrador, stole a few natives, and returned home. The next year he visited, as is supposed, Hudson Strait, but the sea avenged the crime he committed against the people whom it nourished, and devoured him together with his vessel. One of the ships returned home in safety, but nothing was ever heard of Gaspar or his crew.

Gaspar had a brother, Miguel, who begged the king to allow him to go in search of the lost one. Three ships were put under his command, and he sailed for the region about Hudson Strait. On arriving in the vicinity of the probable loss of Gaspar's vessel, the three ships took each certain inlets to examine, agreeing upon a harbor of meeting. Two of them met, after a diligent search. But the ship commanded by Miguel never returned. The sea had, doubtless, swallowed up both him and his men.

There was still another brother of these Cortereals whose name was Vasco. He begged to be sent in search of the missing vessels. But the king's grief was like Jacob's, bereaved of his children. He refused to let Vasco go, but sent armed vessels which searched in vain. Thus ended the arctic explorations in connection with these famous Cortereal brothers—famous more for misfortune than success.

The next expedition was sent out by a company of merchants. Its president was Sebastian Cabot, now an old man, retired on a comfortable pension given by the king "in consideration of the good and acceptable service done by him." Three ships were fitted out, and the command given to Sir Hugh Willoughby, "a valiant gentlemane," under whom was Richard Chancelor, "a man of great estimation for the many good parts of wit in him." The task given them to perform was to find a north-east passage to China and India, which, of course, they expected to perform. They reached Nova Zembla, and were forbidden further progress by the ice. Sir Willoughby returned to the mouth of a river of Lapland, and established his winter-quarters. The ship commanded by Chancelor pushed forward, reached Archangel, and opened the way for trade with Russia. In the spring some Russian fishermen visited the quarters of Sir Willoughby, and found both him and his entire company frozen to death.

But such disasters did not retard other explorations, and we shall next describe *an arctic fever*.

CHAPTER II.

AN ARCTIC GOLD FEVER.

FROBISHER was a learned and able man. He lived in the days of the famous maiden queen of England, Elizabeth. "There were giants" in her reign, and Frobisher was one of them. He was known to fame in his day as a hero in the defeat of the great Spanish Armada, but better known as an arctic explorer.

In early life he became an enthusiastic admirer of Sebastian Cabot and his adventures. He was sure that a north-west passage to India could be found, and that he was the man to find it. He declared that this was the only great thing which remained to be done. No wonder, then, that he gave his time and strength to secure the means of accomplishing it, by converting others to his own faith. Fifteen years he went about preaching "Cathaia" as the promised land, and the north-west as the way to it. Men's ears were dull and their "shoulders" cold toward him. But Frobisher's zeal did not abate. Opposition is the flint which strikes fire from some men. The sparks of enthusiasm which the smitten Frobisher emitted soon set the nation on fire. In 1576 Ambrose Dudley, Earl of Warwick, took up his cause. Under his patronage, three vessels were equipped for the enterprise. They were small affairs after all. The two larger ones were about thirty-five tons each—hardly equal to a coast-wise fishing vessel of the present day—and the third was an attending "pinnace" of ten tons, with a crew of four men. London flocked to the banks of the Thames to see the magnificent exploring fleet sail. Queen Elizabeth, from her window at Greenwich, waved the adventurers a cordial farewell. Not content with this, she sent a gentleman of the court on board the commander's vessel to wish them "happie successe," and to make known her "goode likings of their doings."

The fleet reached, in July, what its commandor called Friesland—probably the southern coast of Greenland. The storm king, who reigned with vigor in this region, forbade their approach to the shore. The pinnace, with its crew, was lost. The "Gabriel," one of the other vessels, considering "discretion the better part of valor," scud ingloriously away and reached England in safety. But Frobisher was true to himself and the enterprise. Calm when the tempest raged with fury, and self-possessed in danger, he inspired his crew with courage, and pressed onward. After many days he reached a dreary shore. The ice soon shut in on the outside, and he pushed forward into a strait to which he gave his own name. He soon espied some strange beings in the water, which he at first thought were porpoises. But they proved to be the Esquimo in their kayaks, or boats. He describes them as "savage people, like to Tartars, having long black hair, broad faces, and flatte noses; the women being marked on the face with blewe streekes downe the cheekes and round the eyes, and wearing bootes made of seal-skins, in shape somewhat resembling the shallops of Spain."

But a sad incident soon interrupted all intercourse between the natives and the strangers. A boat's crew of five men went ashore. Their long absence caused alarm. Trumpets were blown and a cannon was fired to call them back, but in vain. Frobisher hastily and unwisely assumed that they had been violently treated by the Esquimo. His method of revenge was equally unwise and unworthy of his character. He enticed one of them alongside "by the tinkling of a bell." He then "pluckt him up, boat and all." The poor fellow bit his tongue in his rage and despair —"bit it in half by the way."

Frobisher immediately sailed for England, where he was cordially received, though we cannot see what he had accomplished, except to meanly steal a suspected, but unsuspecting, confiding native. A little incident inflamed this cordiality into a wild enthusiasm. Each of the adventurers had brought home some mementos of the exploration, such as flowers, grass, and stones. Frobisher, among other things, presented his friends with specimens of the minerals of the discovered land. One piece, as the story goes, was thrown into the fire. It burned for some time and was then taken out, and "being quenched in a little vinegar it glistened with a bright marquesset of golde." The fever which followed was much like the California "gold fever" of our day, or the diamond fever of the Cape of Good Hope. Frobisher was the lion of the hour, though he seems no way responsible for the public faith in the character of his exhibited minerals. Some "gold-finers" gave opinions to suit the people's wishes, though it is said that a responsible assayer declared that the minerals in question did not contain a particle of the precious ore. But the steam was up, the frenzied train which was to return laden with gold was set in motion, and common sense was run off the track. Both the common people and the queen and her court shared alike in the excitement. The queen commanded that another expedition should be immediately put in readiness. She gave her "loving friend, Martin Frobisher" very full directions for his guidance. In some of these she had an eye to other interests than those of discovery, or even those of golden treasures. She assumed that he would again attempt to land on the stormy coast of "Friesland." So she directed him to take certain condemned persons and leave them there. This little service would relieve her of some troublesome subjects, and he might, as a matter of good-will, "speak with them if possible on his return voyage," giving them at the first such food and weapons as he could well spare, duly instructing them to conduct themselves well and get the good-will of the natives. She further directed him to bring home a few of the natives as specimens. As they were not to be returned, and their consent to the transportation was not to be taken into the account, he was cautioned to be careful where and how they were taken away. There is one excuse for such transactions, which, though poor, is the best we know; it was in accordance with the spirit of the times.

But a better suggestion from the queen was this: He should, if possible, leave some persons to winter on the golden shores of the new country. They were to be instructed to make notes of the state of the country, nature of the air, and observe what time of the year the coast was free from ice. He was to leave them well supplied with food and arms, with a "pinnace," and all other things necessary for their comfort and safety. It does not appear that these last suggestions were acted upon by the explorer. The voyage, however, was made. A little island in what has been known as Frobisher Strait, called Countess of Warwick Isle, was selected, and two hundred tons of the mineral were brought back to the delighted queen, and to her equally delighted people. She called the new land "Meta Incognita," and declared that this voyage greatly increased her hopes that the northwest passage to India would be found.

A new expedition was immediately put in sailing order. One hundred persons, representing various trades and callings, were appointed as settlers. Fifteen vessels were to convey them to the goodly land, Frobisher being commander. Twelve of the ships were to return with the ore, and three were to remain with the colonists.

The expedition sailed, attended with the great expectations of the nation, and a heroism of its men worthy a better aim. Dangers and distresses beset them during the voyage. One vessel, carrying the materials for a large wooden house for the use of the colonists on their arrival, was crushed by icebergs and sunk. Another, under cover of the night, had turned her prow homeward, and sailed for England. The rest were tossed amid "incredible pain and peril." At last a fresh breeze cleared away the ice, and they sailed through a clear sea and soon sighted land, which they supposed to be near Frobisher Strait. But soon this dawn of hope was followed by the darkness of despair. A fog enveloped them, and the vessels were separated, each lost to the proper course. They were driven about at random, while their ears were saluted by the dismal sound of ice crushing against the ship, and of colliding icebergs.

When at last the sky became clear, and the scattered ships reunited, the pilot confessed that he knew not where they were. But Frobisher declared that he knew the coast, and that they were all right. But they failed, after many attempts, to effect a landing. The natives refused to be conciliated, which is not strange, if the policy of former expeditions had been practiced among them. We shall see that later explorers found them kindly disposed.

Thus hindered in his main design, Frobisher fell back upon the passion of his life, and proposed to the other commanders to abandon the colonization scheme and sail on a voyage of discovery. But they rejected the proposal.

Much time had been wasted by these baffled efforts and divided counsels, and their provisions began to fail, while at the same time the vessels were crippled by their icy foe; orders were therefore given to spread sail for home. No settlers had been landed, no gold obtained, not even the deceitful ore of former voyages, and no discoveries had been made.

Thus ended the arctic gold fever. Frobisher fell into neglect, but did not lose his credit, nor the people all of their faith in northern gold mines; for they were slow to believe that he had brought home only "fool's gold"—a micaceous sand—and that "it is not all gold that glitters."

CHAPTER III.

PERILS BY SEA.

FAILURE to secure any substantial success did not restrain the zeal of the queen, nor the spirit of enterprise in other explorers. Immediately on the completion of Frobisher's last voyage, Sir Humphrey Gilbert obtained from Elizabeth full power to undertake a voyage of discovery in the western waters, and to colonize such land as was not already claimed by some Christian sovereign.

Sir Humphrey was a man of mental force and culture. He had studied the north-west passage theory, and given to the world his conclusions in well-written pages. He belonged to a distinguished family, being half-brother to Sir Walter Raleigh. His brother Adrian was already at the head of an influential company for discovery in the north-west.

The queen's terms with Sir Humphrey were very generous. He was to have for his own, forever, all the heathen countries which he might discover, to exercise absolute authority over them, only that they should do homage to his sovereign. Exactly where the distinguishing line was to run between the discover's absolute rule and due homage to England's queen, is not defined in his patent. It was expected probably that both would exist mainly on paper. The queen, however, added a more substantial qualification. Sir Humphrey was to pay her one fifth of all revenues the countries in question might yield. The right of the natives to the land of their fathers was, of course, not considered. It was to be a blessing great enough for them to be owned and governed by the enlightened strangers.

Sir Humphrey left England June, 1583, with five vessels. They had not been long at sea before a fatal sickness occurred among the crew of one of them, and it returned to England. With his remaining fleet the commander landed on Newfoundland and took possession in the name of his queen. A very cool beginning of ownership in the new world, as he was not even the discoverer of this land.

A Saxon miner of the expedition soon reported that he had found a silver mine. But lands and precious ore could not stay the progress of disease. Another vessel was sent home with the sick. The exploring squadron consisted now of the "Delight," the largest and best vessel, the "Golden Hind," and the "Squirrel," a small affair of ten tons, in which the commander himself sailed. With these he put to sea the 20th of August. On the ninth day out a tempest came down upon them, and the "Delight" and "Golden Hind" were driven among rocks and shoals. The "Delight" was on the lead, and struck a quicksand, in which her prow was held firmly. Her stern was soon beaten to fragments by the waves. When the ship struck her boat was afloat at the stern, having been hoisted out the day before to pick up some birds which had been shot from the deck of the vessel. Into this a part of the crew entered. All could not enter; and the question, severely testing the unselfish heroism of every one, was pressed upon them: Who shall remain by the ship? Captain Browne, who had been transferred from the "Swallow" into the "Delight," at once set the noble example of preferring the safety of others to himself. Others followed this example, and sixteen only, including Mr. Clarke, the master, escaped in the boat. The captain and one hundred men calmly awaited their fate, and perished on the breaking up of the vessel.

Those who were in the boat were scarcely to be congratulated. Overladen, and without provisions, they drifted before the furious tempest. The nights were starless, and the darkness awful. At the end of two days it seemed that the boat could not longer float in the heavy sea, and one of the sailors, by the name of Headly, proposed that they draw lots, and that the four getting the four shortest lots be thrown overboard, to increase the chance of the safety of the rest. To this proposal the master gave an emphatic "No!" "We will all live," he exclaimed, "or die together!"

Four days passed away, and no relief came. On the fifth, Headly and one other man died. All except Clarke were in despair, and cried for death to end their misery. He calmly exhorted them still to trust the Divine arm and hope for deliverance. On the sixth day, when hope seemed to be gone, he boldly declared that the morrow would bring deliverance, adding, "If it does not, throw me overboard." About noon of the seventh day the shore of Newfoundland was seen. In the middle of the afternoon they landed, with difficulty creeping from the boats. Their first act, most fittingly, was to fall on their knees and thank God for their deliverance. The stronger then brought water from a brook, and all quenched their thirst. They found near them a good supply of wild berries, and, building a hut of boughs, they remained on shore a few days and were sufficiently recruited to row quietly along the shore, landing for water and their supply of fruit. Soon a Spanish whaler picked them up and landed them at a port in the Bay of Biscay. They traveled on foot through France, and arrived in England the latter part of 1583, to tell the sad result of their hopefully begun expedition.

We left the "Golden Hind" in the midst of the storm which proved so disastrous to the Delight. She beat off from the rocks among which they were entangled and reached the open sea. All of both vessels now united in requesting the commander to return to England. In no wise daunted by his misfortunes, he agreed to do this, after securing a pledge from his men to sail with him on another north-west expedition the next spring.

Having spread their sails for the homeward passage, Sir Humphrey several times left the "Squirrel" to spend an hour on board the "Golden Hind." As his little craft was overloaded, both below and on deck, and was not considered safe, the captain of the "Hind" besought him to remain in his ship. "No," says the noble commander, "if there are perils ahead I will share them with those in whose company I have passed through so many." Once he came on board the "Hind" to have an injured foot dressed by its surgeon. His condition offered a good occasion for him to remain. But neither his own comfort, nor a feast prepared by the Hind's officers and crew, could entice him from his post of danger. Soon after his return a storm arose. In the afternoon of the day it commenced Sir Humphrey was seen sitting in the stern of his little imperiled craft with a book in his hand. He shouted, "Courage, my lads, we are as near heaven at sea as on land." They were his last known words. That night the "Squirrel's" light was seen for a few hours glimmering in the darkness, and rising and falling with the waves. Soon that disappeared, and the career of the brave little ship, with its noble commander and crew, was closed. The "Golden Hind" returned alone, to anticipate in part the recital of the sad tale of the rescued boat's crew.

The next English explorer, John Davis, was more chary of perils by sea. He was willing, however, in order to find the much-desired golden gate, or rather the north-west gate to the gold and diamonds of the east, to subject himself to a reasonable amount of peril.

Some "divers worshipful merchants of London," not deterred by treasures already lost in similar adventures, fitted out and put Davis in command of two vessels—the "Sunshine" and "Moonshine."

They sailed from the Thames in June, 1585, and in six weeks they were on the coast of Greenland. Their early and first peril was from a dense, long-continued fog bank. During its gloomy darkness they were affrighted by terrific grindings and loud roarings, which greatly puzzled them. They could not be the crash of thunder, nor the sound of distant waterfalls breaking through icy restraints. But they were soon able to explain these intimidating sounds, for the grinding together of huge masses of ice soon became a familiar, if not a pleasant, sight and sound.

When the fog cleared away, and Davis and his men were able to view the shore, they were not greatly comforted. He says: "The country was as dreary as it is possible to conceive. The loathsome view of the shore, and the irksome noise of the ice, were such that they bred strange conceits among us, so that we supposed the place to be waste, and void of any sensible or vegetable creatures. So we named the same—*Desolation*."

But they found even these regions not all desolation. Sailing west, he discovered a clear sea, with "green and pleasant isles bordering on the shore." Even the natives smiled upon them, and they entered into trade for furs.

A favoring wind springing up, Davis spread his

sails and steered across an expanse of water until they rounded a cape in great spirits, calling the point of land "The Cape of God's Mercy." There was no ice, and the commander thought that the way "to Cathay" was found at last. "Why," he exclaims, "the water is of the very color, nature, and quality of the ocean!" Sailing on over two hundred miles in the happy delusion, he was confirmed in it by their arrival at a cluster of inviting islands. But the old fog banks soon turned the current of their thoughts. A storm arose and the sea became boisterous. Not liking fogs and storms, Davis quickly sailed to England, hoping to come into those regions again another day.

Twice again he visited the same coast, making surveys of the western coast of Greenland, and making the world acquainted with the waters now known as Davis Strait, and thus opening a wide door for those who might follow. He had not, however, filled his ships with gold, nor sailed to Cathay through the icy north, and so he gave way to other and newly-risen stars.

CHAPTER IV.

ICE-BOUND.

WHILE England was sending her heroic men to arctic regions, other nations were on the alert. Among them none were more enterprising than the Hollanders. We give an example of the heroism of the great Dutch commanders.

In 1596 William Barentz sailed into the waters between Spitzbergen and Nova Zembla. It was his third voyage into the frozen regions, yet the perils he was now called to face were enough to make even his well-tried courage fail. The ice drifts came crowding around them until it had made escape impossible. He says: "It made all the hair of our heads to rise upright with fear, and forced us, in great cold, poverty, misery, and grief, to stay all that winter." But they strove manfully against such a dreaded necessity.

On the 11th of September all hope of relief was given up, and a council was called in which the question was discussed how they might best defend themselves against wild beasts and the cold. They finally determined to build a hut upon the land, and "so to commit themselves into the tuition of God."

This being determined, the next question was,

Of what shall our hut be made? No trees grew on the shore upon which they had been cast. Looking about for material, they stumbled upon a good quantity of drift-wood. They joyfully regarded this needed article as coming through the direct interposition of God. Well did Barentz write: "We were much comforted, being in good hope that God would show us some further favor. The wood served us not only to build our house, but also to burn during the whole winter. Without it, without all doubt, we had died there miserably with extreme cold."

They at once set to work to build their house. But they had not learned arctic house building. Some put the nails they purposed to use between their lips, and when they removed them the skin was taken too, and the pain was as if they had been burned. The bears, also, troubled them. The reader will wonder at this, as he will at this party's hut constructing and other management, when he has followed later explorers into the arctic regions. White men had not yet learned of the simple Esquimo how to live amid perpetual ice and intense cold, and to regard the visit of the bear as the good gift of the Great Spirit. A bear *troubling* a whole ship's crew, when his fur and meat were just the needed articles, and then walking audaciously away, would have made an Esquimo woman shrug her shoulders, and, with her people's peculiar laugh, to say, "White men all same as boys."

When the hut was finished the needed stores

were removed to it from the ship. All this time the open water was within "arrow-shot" of the vessel! Dr. Kane would have found a way to "cut her out," and thus to have escaped.

When the cracks in their house were chinked with the weed they found about the shore, and all their goods removed from the vessel, they "set up the dial and made the clock strike."

It was now November, the sun had ceased to appear above the horizon, and the long winter set in. Regulations for the company were adopted, and each assigned his daily round of duty. The dignity of the officers was duly regarded, the master and pilot being exempted from cutting wood and "such rude labors." Habits which concerned health were wisely regarded. The surgeon contrived to make a bath tub of a wine-pipe, in which all bathed in turn, and at stated times, and were much benefited. Traps were sometimes set for the foxes that came skulking round; foxes, however, it would seem, were too cunning to be caught.

The snow shut them up for days together, and the cold stopped their clock, so that the slow-moving hours were counted only by the hour-glass. Their only light was the economically supplied fire. Ice formed in their sleeping berths, and the smoke and impure air were continual annoyances. Linen froze the instant it was taken from hot water. The painful stillness without was occasionally broken by the thunder of icebergs as they were rent asunder, or brought into sudden contact. At other times the bark of the fox or the growl of the bear would fall on their ears. When not employed in cooking many spent their time in bed.

No wonder, in view of all these discomforts, at the dismal tone of the following extract from the commander's diary! "It was foul weather again, with an easterly wind and extreme cold, almost not to be endured; whereupon we looked pitifully one upon the other, being in great fear that if the extremity of the cold grew to be more and more, we should all die there with cold; for what fire we made it would not warm us. Yea, and our sack, which is so hot, was frozen very hard, so that when we were every man to have his part we were forced to melt it in the fire. We had of this, every second day, about half a pint to a man. At other times we had water, which agreed not well with the cold, and we needed not to cool it with snow or ice; but we were forced to melt it out of the snow."

On the 7th of December they went on board the ship, and brought to the hut "some coals." Of these they made a cheerful fire, in which they for a while rejoiced. But the escaping gas gave them all a sudden dizziness, and one fainted. Evidently they came near being suffocated. The door was opened, and they felt better; and then "a glass of wine was served out to each man, to recover him completely."

On the 19th of November they tried to get some cheer from the fact that the time of the sun's absence was half expired. The seamen's shoes had now frozen so that they could not wear them, and they made them slippers of skins, and wore several pair of socks at once.

Their stock of wood was expended by the middle of January, but it was replenished by weary digging in the snow. Going to the ship one day, a fox was discovered in the cabin; he was caught, carried to the hut, his flesh eaten, and his skin made into warm slippers.

On "Twelfth Night"—a national holiday—they tried to be merry. From their scanty allowance of wine they had saved an extra portion for this occasion. When mentioning this wine they add: "We fancied ourselves at home in Holland." If they were indebted to the wine for this "fancy," wine, true to its character, was to them a cruel "mocker." We think this was even so, for they "soaked biscuit in wine, drank to the three kings of Cologne, and comforted themselves as if they had been at a great feast." They drew lots to see who should be king of Nova Zembla, and the lot fell to the gunner. It is said, in fact, that they were as happy as if they had been in their own houses among the dykes of Holland. But where wine presides at the board, headache and sleepless nights follow, and "sweet home" "dissolves like the baseless fabric of a vision."

The next few days were very stormy, and, no doubt, very "blue." They remained in their hut and heard the foxes fearlessly running over the roof. The bears passed in and out of their deserted ship. The cold grew more intense. With their feet to the fire, their socks burned before the flesh felt the warmth, and their backs were covered with frost.

On the 24th of January three of the men, going to the sea-side toward the south, caught a glimpse, as they thought, of the sun above the horizon. But their commander doubted the good news, as the sun was not due by his reckoning. Many days following were densely cloudy, and they obtained no additional evidence of his welcome return.

Though the cheerful sun came not to the ice-bound and suffering wretches, death entered their abode. On the 26th they carried one of their number out to his deep-snow grave. He had long been sick, and now, around his cold remains, they read "certain chapters from God's Word," and mournfully chanted their psalms.

A polar bear, which had, no doubt, during the winter, observed the ways of these strangers, and not being attacked, very naturally resolved to attack them. He came boldly up to their dwelling. They attempted to shoot him, but their "matchlocks" missed fire. The bear, despising the arms-length fighting of the white faces, made a rush at the door of the hut. The men rushed in, and held it fast on the inside, having in their flight, dropped the bar by which they usually secured it. After trying to force it the bear walked away, but soon returned, mounted the roof, and roared furiously for admission. The terror of the inmates was now very great. If he should break through, there would be just one too many in their close quarters. But the bear contented himself, by necessity, as he could not break through, with "sound and fury," and went away.

On the 4th of May the open sea came within five hundred paces of the ship. They decided, however, not to wait the chances of being able to float their ship, but resolved to venture their safety in their boats. They had a voyage before them of many hundred miles over a cold and stormy sea. They repaired their two boats, and, on the 13th of June, the forlorn party, twelve in number, left that "desert, irksome, fearful, and cold country." They were destitute of every comfort, and of almost all the common necessities of existence. Soon three of them died, and were committed to the deep!

After many weary days they came in sight of a long-desired cape. When the good news that the cape was in sight was shouted from the deck, Barentz was below examining a chart which De Veer, one of his companions, had made of the coasts they had seen on their voyage. He had become very weary, and desired to be carried on deck that he might see the land.

Not long after the sad tidings was communicated from the other boat that Claes Andriz was dying. "I shall soon follow Andriz!" said Barentz. "De Veer," he added, "give me something to drink."

He took the cup from De Veer, drank, fell back into his arms, and died.

The company in the other boat were, at the same time, closing the eyes in death of Andriz.

The two boats were now in an almost desperate condition. Their commander had been their principal navigator, from his superior knowledge and experience. His courage and hopeful temper had been the inspiration of their flagging spirits. They, however, manfully contended against the fearful difficulties; and in September, having been nearly three months on board their frail boats, they reached the coast of Lapland. They say: "We now saw some trees on the river side, which comforted us and made us glad, as if we then had come into a new world; for in all the time we had been out we had not seen any trees."

Having arrived at Coola, which we understand to be a port of Lapland, they finished a voyage of eleven hundred and forty-three miles, and put their boats in the "Merchant's House, as a sign and token of their deliverance."

In a few weeks they sailed for Amsterdam in a Dutch ship. They appeared before their friends in the dress they had worn during their perils, and were received as those who, being lost, were found. They were honored and feasted. The common people heard their story with wonder, and they were invited to repeat it before the ministers of foreign States at the Hague.

CHAPTER V.

SET ADRIFT.

THE next prominent candidate for the perils and honors of arctic exploration was Henry Hudson. The Muscovy wealth-seeking company first sent him out in 1607. His orders were to penetrate directly to the North Pole. Hudson seems to have answered, in spirit: I will try, gentlemen. He reached, by the way of Spitzbergen, the latitude of 81½°, an approach to the point to which he was sent not much exceeded at any time since, until the last American expedition under Captain Hall. He then coasted awhile about Spitzbergen, and came home declaring that there was an insurmountable ice barrier across the way to the pole in that direction. This declaration has never been proved false.

He was next sent to find a north-east passage to India, a result much desired by his employers, as, in their estimation, it would be equivalent to the discovery of great riches. In the spirit of *I'll try*, he sailed in 1608. He made the coast of Nova Zembla after hard fighting with the Ice King, into whose domains he had dared to penetrate. Being defeated by this venerable sovereign of the whole northern region, he returned home and testified that a north-east passage to India in ships had no existence, except in the fancies and wishes of certain merchants who would make haste to be rich. This testimony of the brave sailor stands unimpeached to this day. Hudson's sailors declared that while at one time out in a boat, during this voyage, they saw a mermaid. They did not, however, catch her and bring her to England. So a grave doubt rests upon their testimony.

The Dutch did not believe the faithful statement of Hudson, but would have him try the north-east passage again. He did so, in 1609, and was warned off, as before, by the grim Ice King; he obeyed, and turned his ships toward the American coast, taking care to steer away from the regions controlled by his frosty majesty. He arrived at what is now New York harbor, and discovered the beautiful river to which his name has been attached to this day. This was exploring to good purpose, whether it satisfied the merchants of Holland or not.

The next year a rich company of London merchants started him off again. Strange to say, the explorers again confronted their old enemy on the south-east coast of Iceland, where they dropped anchor. They were beset with fog, and soon found themselves beset also by "bergs" and "packs," the skirmishers of the Ice King. They wisely took the hint and left. Going round to the west coast they caught a fine lot of fish. Here they saw Mount Hecla in a blaze, the brightness of its fires lighting up the land and sea, and sparkling from the eternal snows.

They made a harbor, where they killed a good supply of sea-fowl. Attempting to sail, they were driven into another harbor, where they found warm springs, in which they bathed; some of them were hot enough to boil their fowl in.

They now sailed away for Greenland, and coasted along its north-west side, seeing many whales. Scudding before the wind, they went west of north, and encountered great quantities of floating ice, on which were numerous seals. Hudson was carried along with the current which bore the ice, and after fruitless attempts to get free from it gave up the attempt, and yielded to feelings of discouragement. He called his men together, showed them his chart, and called their attention to the fact that they had sailed a hundred leagues further than any of their countrymen had done. He then submitted the question to them whether to go further or to return.

The council thus called seems to have been divided and insubordinate. The commander, as might have been supposed, was obliged to assume the responsibility, which he did by pushing forward. He soon after discovered some islands under which he found shelter. Going ashore they found game and drift-wood, and, being refreshed and encouraged, called them the "Isles of God's Mercy."

Sailing again, and borne hither and thither by the varying ice-laden current, he was at last carried much to the west of what he expected by the rush of the tide into the great bay which bears his name. Gaining the shelter of another island, a boat was sent ashore. They found upon it herds of deer—though their clumsy guns failed to bring down any—abundance of wild fowl, and some herbage and scurvy-grass. The boat explorers were called on board by an alarm-gun, as a storm was coming on. The crew, having been consulted before, now *tendered* their advice. They wanted to stay here and recruit. But Hudson was elated by the idea of the vast sea into which he had just entered, and thinking, perhaps, that the way to "Cathay" was at last open to him, weighed anchor and bore away. The muttering storm of discontent among the crew, so long gathering, began to break out in fitful gusts. Hudson at once assumed the stern authority of the ship-master, and degraded two of his officers, the mate and boatswain, making Bylot mate and Wilson boatswain. In doing this he is accused of acting under the influence of a spirit of revenge for provocations a long time before given by the degraded men. This seems to us unlikely, his own safety forbidding the master to take such a time to pay off old grudges.

After some exciting adventures, in which the crew and their commander came into collision, they began to look about for winter-quarters. It was November, the nights were long and cold, and the snow every-where deep. Drawing their ship up near the shore they were soon frozen in. Their provisions were low, and all were put on a short allowance. The crew, ever forward with their advice, counseled the building of a house on shore. This seems to have been good advice, but Hudson flatly refused to have it done. A most unfortunate state of irritability had been fostered between the two parties. Some time later, when the commander saw the necessity of a house on shore, he commanded the carpenter to build one. "I neither can nor will," was that officer's reply. Hudson attempted to strike him, and hurled at him sharp words. "I know my duty; I am no *house* carpenter," rejoined the carpenter.

This, as it may be seen, is possibly a one-sided account. It does not accord with the later, noble conduct of the carpenter to his commander.

After further delay the house was built, but in such a manner that it proved of no use.

The winter was a severe one, and their provisions were nearly exhausted. Sickness, of course, prevailed, and much suffering was experienced. They, however, shot a great many wild fowl, and procured from beneath the snow some moss and buds, all of which were eaten and acted favorably in staying the progress of the scurvy.

In the spring the Esquimo visited them, and a trade was entered into for furs in exchange for trinkets.

Hudson now prepared to return home. With a sorrowful heart, and, it is said, with tearful eyes, he distributed to the company a portion of the small remnant of their provisions, not more than enough to last ten days. He remarked in giving it out: "I also give you *a bill of return*, so that if you ever get home you may show it."

A short time after they caught "fourscore small fish," which, though but little among so many, ought to have impressed them that they might look for a providential supply.

They set sail, we may be assured, with heavy hearts. But a feeling worse than that of heaviness was indulged by many. They dropped anchor before clearing the bay—now Hudson Bay—when the rebellious spirit on board assumed the form of open violence. The mutineers took an occasion, when officers and men were widely scattered about the ship, to seize the commander as he was leaving the cabin and to tie his hands behind him.

"What do you mean to do?" he demanded.

"You will know when we get you into the boat," was the reply.

The rebels, who were strong in numbers, were armed, and presented deadly weapons to the friends of Hudson. Some of the sick boldly denounced the mutineers, and told them that they would find England, if they arrived there, a worse place than their present one.

Hudson and eight sick men were violently dragged into a small shallop, with only two days' provisions. The carpenter, though regarded as a friend of Hudson, was not put into the boat with him. When he saw the fate that had been devised for his commander, he denounced, in no smooth terms, the rebels, and boldly declared that he preferred his company in the boat to theirs in the ship. His noble conduct seems to have subdued in a measure even his wicked shipmates, and they allowed him to take his chest, musket, powder and shot, a few cooking utensils, and some other necessaries, and a small addition to the stock of provisions.

The shallop was then set adrift, while the ship hoisted sails and bore away. Doubtless the mutineers watched the victims of their great crime, until they were lost in the rapidly increasing distance.

Night threw her mantle over the separated parties. The morning dawned with a clouded sky and stormy winds. All day the gale drove fields of ice over the open waters, and rendered navigation impossible, while the great icebergs went plunging through the deep, or fiercely rushed together like angry gladiators. Hudson and his companions were, without doubt, lost on that fearful day; yet no messenger, even in the form of a faintly intimating relic, ever appeared to tell the story of the time and circumstances of their last moments. Posterity drops a tear over their watery graves, and history perpetuates the memory of Hudson in the name of the bay which he discovered.

The guilty ship's company steered homeward, keeping the headlands in view. On one of these they landed to secure a needed supply of sea-fowls. Meeting on shore peaceably disposed Esquimo, they began to trade with them, exchanging trinkets for furs and fresh provisions. At one time a boat having articles for such purposes on board, went ashore. Green, who seems to have been the chief villain of the gang, ventured, with others, away from the boat, and mixed freely with the natives, showing goods. Pricket only was left in the boat. Seeing the strangers thus off their guard, and tempted, no doubt, by the coveted trinkets, a savage attacked Pricket with a deadly weapon. A desperate struggle ensued, Pricket finally killing the assailant. A general conflict at once commenced, in which four of Green's party, fighting their way to the boat, reached it only after receiving serious wounds. The remaining one jumped into the sea from a rocky point and swam to the boat after it pushed off, seizing its stern, and begging to be taken in; his companions, it seems, being regardless of his fate. The savages persisted in their attack, and were beaten off with a pike and hatchet. Green was killed on the spot. The rest reached the ship, but three died of their wounds. The cry of the blood of their murdered commander was speedily avenged.

The ship was now insufficiently manned, and there were no relieving parties to go ashore for birds. With great labor they killed and salted three hundred. They then sailed out of the strait, and bore away for England. The last ringleader in the rebellion died on the voyage. They reached their own country, after being driven to the very extremity of starvation, a wretched, guilty company as ever returned from an arctic exploration.

Their suffering, miserable condition seems to have turned aside the sword of justice, usually so quick in old England to punish crimes like theirs, and they were not arrested. Indeed, two of them sailed in the next arctic expedition.

CHAPTER VI.

SHIPWRECK AND ESCAPE.

HUDSON'S discovery of a great body of water, extending farther west than previous voyagers had sailed, created great excitement. Much controversy was the result, some contending that the highway to India, so long sought, led out of it. But it was a long time, as we shall see, before much additional knowledge was obtained of regions lying farther west.

In 1616 William Baffin discovered the bay which bears his name. It is a vast extent of water, eight hundred miles long and three hundred wide. Its discovery was a full compensation to the world for the failures of many previous expeditions. Its waters have yielded great treasures to the adventurous whalemen. Baffin barely missed opening to navigation Lancaster Sound. He sailed by and observed its entrance, but what lay beyond remained unknown for two hundred years.

While the English and other nations were pushing their explorations westward from Hudson and Baffin Bay, the Russians were, with equal energy, surveying the Arctic coast-line of their own extended possessions. From time to time expeditions were sent eastward from the White

Sea, discovering the rivers and bays along the Siberian coast, to the Lena. Other expeditions sailed west from Bering Strait to the Kolyma and Lena. The sufferings of these adventurers were very great. Their vessels were small affairs, varying from ten to fifty tons, and in the means of comfort and safety of life which they afforded compared unfavorably with the pleasure yachts of our bays. This is true of all the exploring vessels of these early times.

Passing the smaller expeditions which, in their aggregate discoveries, opened extended lines of sea-coast, we present more fully that of the famous Russian commander, Captain Vitus Bering. In 1728 he was given the command of two vessels, the "Fortuna" and "Gabriel." He sailed from the mouth of the Kamchatka River in July, and, coasting northward, reached a point in Bering Strait where the land swept off to the westward. This, he assumed, proved the separation of Asia and America, thus settling one of the great questions for which the voyage had been undertaken. This done, Bering returned home. He was afraid of the winter and its Ice King, and seems to have cared more for ease and safety than great exploits.

Bering's timid policy lost him no favor with his Government. He was advanced to the rank of commander, and his lieutenants given commissions as captains. Supply depots were established on the Kamchatka coast, the exploring interest was kept up by the discussion of various projects, until, in 1741, Bering again made the long overland journey from St. Petersburgh to Avatcha, Kamchatka. His expedition from this port consisted of two vessels—the "St. Peter," commanded by himself, and the "St. Paul," Chirikoff, captain. They sailed on the 4th of June, and on the 20th of June the vessels were separated by a storm, and were not again in company. About the middle of July the "St. Paul" anchored off the American coast. The long-boat, with eleven armed men, was sent ashore. Anxiously, for six days, the commander waited in vain for its return. Then a smaller boat, with six men, was sent to search for it, but neither of the boats returned, and the fate of the men remained a matter of conjecture. A sad intimation, however, of their end was given by the appearance the next day of two canoes filled with savages. On seeing the Russians crowding their vessels' deck, they made a fierce outcry and paddled swiftly away.

Having now no boats, Chirikoff sailed back to Avatcha, having on his voyage lost twenty-one of his seventy men; four, among whom was a celebrated naturalist, Crozere, died of scurvy.

Bering, in the "St. Peter," had a more eventful career. The first land he made on the American coast was examined by two boats in reference to a supply of fresh water. One of them, commanded by Steller, met a small company of the natives, who were peaceably disposed. They consisted of men only, who had been on a fishing excursion. They had captured a whale, and offered the strangers some of the blubber, urging them to eat.

Though the result of these boat excursions was favorable to a longer stay, Bering hoisted sail and put to sea. A violent storm, which lasted seventeen days, overtook him, and he was driven far to the southward. To add to his disasters the scurvy broke out among the crew. A good supply, freely eaten, of the whale's flesh which the Esquimo tendered might have prevented this. As it was, the men were generally disabled, and many died. The steersman was upheld by a comrade on either side, both about as feeble as he. When the ship's watches were changed, it was but one set of invalids succeeding another. A cold rain, by which they had been drenched, was succeeded by sleet and snow. The nights grew longer and the darkness more intense, while, at the same time, they became entangled in a scattered group of islands. The supply of water was small, and the quality poor. The sailors were at last so few in number and so weak that they were unable longer to manage the ship, and she was for several days driven by the wind or drifted by the current. On the 4th of November the crew rallied, and attempted to regain command of the ship, and put her prow to the westward. While struggling to accomplish this they were thrilled with joy at the sight, in the distance, of snow-capped mountains. They knew not whether they were those of their own Kamchatka or some far away island. Before they could reach the shore the long, dark, and intensely cold night set in. During its weary, slow-passing hours, the cordage supporting one side of the masts gave way, rendering the larger sails useless. Thus crippled, and about destitute of water, they determined, at all risks, to run the vessel ashore. For this purpose, when the morning dawned, they hoisted some light sail upon the quivering masts. Seeing the ship drifting upon a rocky reef, they threw out an anchor; but the cable soon parted, and she struck twice upon it. A moment after, however, a huge wave lifted her up, and bore her safely over the reef into calm water with a sandy bottom. They were but a short distance from the shore. They were in a land-locked harbor, and had been driven in through a merciful providence by the winds and waves through the narrow and only possible entrance. They rested until noon of the next day. Bering had been for some time confined to his berth with the scurvy. Waxel, who succeeded to the command, and Steller, surgeon and naturalist, now landed to explore the country. It was dreary enough. There were no trees inviting them to a shelter under their intertwining branches; no Esquimo huts offered their simple hospitality. One feature only was cheering: there was a beautiful stream of pure water, which the Ice King, forbidden by the Great King, had not yet touched by his congealing wand. It was murmuring a plaintive welcome to the forlorn strangers as it rushed over its rocky bed.

Waxel and Steller found some excavations in

the banks of this stream, which they resolved to cover with the sails of the ship as the best temporary provision they could make for the sick. This they did, and in a few days attempted to bring them ashore. Some died the moment they reached the open air; others died on board the boat, and some immediately on landing.

These deceased comrades were laid in a solemn row on the shore to await a kindly burial; but their bodies were instantly attacked by rapacious foxes, who mangled some of them before they could be interred.

On the second day of the removals, Bering was brought ashore and placed in a hut by himself. He was tenderly carried by his men from the boat, and his necessities were met as far as the painful circumstances allowed. But he rapidly sunk under his disease, his age and temperament being against him. He became delirious as his life drew to a close, imagining his friends to be his enemies, and not permitting some of them to come into his presence. He indulged the strange fancy of scooping up the loose sand near his bed and covering his feet with it. He was very angry if his attendants removed it. He was finally left to gratify this strange desire, and he sunk into the arms of death, half buried by his own hands. His name was given to the island, which has become to all nations, and all succeeding generations, his monument.

No other officer died, though several others were at times attacked with the prevailing disease.

But the disasters of the wretched company were not ended. A few days after the burial of their commander a violent storm arose. The sea broke over the reef girding their harbor, and rolled vast waves to the shore. Their ship, their only dependence for escape, swung uneasily at her mooring. She had lost two anchors, and one only remained. None but men situated as they were can appreciate the anxiety with which they watched her unequal contest with the mighty sea. All day of the 29th of September she bravely clung to her anchor. The night, long, dark, and fearfully tempestuous, set in, and left the shipwrecked islanders to watch through its hours in torturing uncertainty.

When, at last, the morning lighted up the shore, the ship was seen upon the beach, buried deep in the sand, and sadly shattered by the waves. A large part of their provisions, which, strange to say, had not been removed to the shore, was lost.

The party began now to look about them most carefully. They soon learned that they were upon an island. They found drift-wood, by digging under the snow, for improving their huts and for fuel. This was a timely supply, without which they must have perished. The blue and white foxes, which annoyed them on landing, and sacrilegiously attacked their dead, were glad to keep out of their way, and were made to help largely in supplying their table. "The sea-beaver," as they called another of the island animals, they ate only when hard pressed for food, as their flesh was hard and "stringy." They even turned up their noses at the flesh of the seal, pronouncing its smell and taste decidedly disagreeable, (which proves that they were not driven very near to the verge of starvation.) The "sea-lion" they pronounced excellent. The walrus was much relished, the flesh being "like beef," and the young ones tasting like "the best veal;" they used their fat for butter. They even salted several hogsheads of this walrus meat for their voyage of escape, if they ever made one. A part of the small remains of the provision saved from the ship was put away for the same purpose.

At a time in the winter when they seemed in some danger of falling short of provisions a whale came ashore near their huts. They found its flesh, when separated by boiling from the fat, good eating. In the spring another whale stranded upon their beach. Thus God wonderfully provided for these shipwrecked islanders.

It was now April, 1742; the snow had melted, and the wreck and drift-wood were uncovered. They began to debate the question, How shall we escape from the island?—a question, one would think, hard to answer. Waxel proposed tearing the old wreck to pieces, and the construction of a smaller vessel of the materials. All concurred in the proposal. But the carpenters of the expedition, three in number, had died during the winter. Here was a serious perplexity. In the emergency a Cossack, by the name of Sawa, who had worked awhile in a Russian navy-yard, stepped forward and said he would try. The commander suggested the dimensions, forty feet long and thirteen broad. The vessel was begun in May, and on the 10th of August it was launched and named the "St. Peter." It had one mast and one deck. A cabin was built on the after-part, and a cook-house on the fore-part. The shot and iron of the wreck were used as ballast. Arrangements were made for four oars amid-ships. Favored by calm weather after the launching, they hung the rudder, put in the mast, "bent the sails," took the provisions and the few valuables their shipwreck had left them, adding no small amount of furs collected on the island. Having built their sailing vessel, they added to it a boat large enough to carry nine persons.

Seldom have men reduced to so desperate a condition risen to one so hopeful. On the 16th of August they bid adieu to their island home, manned their oars, rowed over the reef, and, when well out to sea, hoisted sail and steered for Kamchatka. Their vessel behaved well, to the joy of all and the honor of Sawa. On the 27th they safely entered the port from whence they had sailed with such high hopes fifteen months before. Chirikoff's ship, though it had been out in search of them, was there. They were, of course, warmly welcomed, and became the heroes of the hour. Sawa was regarded as the rescuer of the company, and was made a nobleman of inferior order.

Thus ended the last expedition under Bering—its shipwreck and escape.

Having thus shown the progress of arctic discovery into the middle of the eighteenth century, we will pause to glance at some of its moral and religious results.

CHAPTER VII.

ARCTIC MISSION-WORK.

WE have related in an early chapter the fact that a Danish settlement in Greenland immediately followed the pioneer voyagers. We have noted, too, the history of a Roman Catholic mission which attended it, and given passing notice of the remarkable circumstance that the entire colony, with its mission, was mysteriously blotted out. We devote now a few pages to the revival of the mission-work there by better teachers with a purer faith.

In the early part of the eighteenth century a Norwegian boy by the name of Hans Egede listened to the wonderful legends of his fatherland with deep interest. The stories concerning the Zenos especially impressed him. Mixed with tales of their shipwreck on the Greenland shore were vague accounts of heroic Christian efforts for the conversion of its heathen people. The lack of reliable information as to what had been done afforded a broad field for the exercise of his lively imagination. His desire to preach Christ in Greenland grew with his increasing years, and became the staple of his talk. But the Church received his suggestions coldly, and the world laughed at him. Being thus restrained, he became parish minister at Vogen, in the north of Norway, was married, and had four children. But the fiery zeal of his youth for Greenland and its perishing heathen burned with unabated intensity. His wife even opposed it, but Egede had no rest. "He that forsaketh not all that he hath for my sake is not worthy of me," seemed ever ringing in his ears. He spread the matter before God in earnest daily prayer. His wife's objections were first removed, and she became an ardent co-operator, declaring she was ready to forsake all and to face every toil and danger. He pressed his suit upon the Mission College, and was rejected with some assurance of future aid. He next appeared before the king himself. Royal ears were opened to his impassioned appeal, difficulties gave way, ten thousand dollars were raised, a small vessel, called the "Hope," purchased, and Hans Egede with his family landed in Greenland in the summer of 1721. He chose for his first station a small island near the mouth of the Baal River, in latitude about 65°.

Strange to say, Egede, with all his seemingly God-inspired zeal and his undoubted Christian heroism, mistook at first, at least, the vital duty of a true apostolic missionary—that of preaching Christ. He began his instructions with the story of the creation, and endeavored thus indirectly to prepare his hearers for the story of the cross. His Christian spirit conciliated the natives, and subdued the opposition of prejudice which first attended his good offices. Still none were converted. He toiled on ten long years, patiently praying and waiting.

In 1731 Egede seems to have begun to have some fruit, for several were baptized. Two of these were taken to Denmark by the colonists, and their story awakened a deep interest in the minds of the devoted Moravians of that country. Their story was reported to the congregation at Herrnhut. Matthew Stach arose and said: "Send me to Greenland; the Lord hath called me." His cousin, Christian Stach, added, "Me, too, hath God commanded to go!" Christian David, a veteran teacher, united with them in the noble enterprise.

The congregation which said to these brethren, "Go; God be with you, and bless you!" were a poor persecuted people. They had only their blessing to give.

These three started for Copenhagen, a district of five hundred miles, afoot, carrying their entire worldly substance on their backs. The day before starting they received an unsolicited donation, and while this lasted they refused all proffered charities by the way.

When they arrived at Copenhagen they were regarded as fanatics. Count Pless inquired of them how they would support themselves in Greenland.

"With our hands," was the prompt reply.

"How will you find shelter and a home?"

"We will build a house and live in it."

"But there is no timber in Greenland!"

"Then we will dig a hole in the ground and live in that!"

"No," replied the count, "that will be too bad. Here's money enough to buy lumber for a house; carry the material for your home with you, and God bless you!"

They arrived in Greenland in April, 1733, and built their humble house on the mainland near the island on which Egede had so long toiled. They put up, also, a house in which to receive the natives who might visit them. They called their locality Herrnhut. Scarcely had they become settled before the small pox swept away large numbers of the natives, and prostrated the missionaries. While thus burdened they were cheered by the unexpected coming to join them in their labors of two of their brethren from home, Beck and Boenish. These so diligently and aptly applied themselves to the Esquimo language that they soon printed for native use copies of the Lord's Prayer, the Ten Commandments, and the Apostles' Creed. But they were unsuccessful in hunting, not having learned the ways of the natives in this respect. Their stock of provisions was much reduced, so that there remained for the entire mission only a barrel and a half of oatmeal, with no apparent resource when that should be eaten. The Esquimo, seeing their reduced state, watched for the moment when starvation should make them helpless to utterly destroy them. But the men of God cried unto him, and in the spring of 1736 ample supplies were sent by an unknown benefactor in Holland. Having thus enough to eat for the present, more laborers and more mouths to feed came from their home. In the summer following, the mother of Matthew Stach, a widow, and his two sisters, joined the mission. The mother immediately relieved the men of the burden of domestic affairs, and the sisters—Rosina, twenty-two years old, and Anna twelve—showed great aptness in learning the native language, and soon became efficient spiritual helpers. For two years from this time this united, unflinching company of eight Christians endured all manner of annoyances from those whom they came to tell of Jesus and his love. Hideous howlings saluted their ears by night. Whenever they went out they were mocked, pelted with stones, and threatened with death. Their boats were loosened from their moorings and set adrift.

Thus affairs stood when a party of South Greenland natives arrived at the settlement. One of them, Kayarnak, was at one time sitting near Beck while he was attempting the translation of the Gospel of Matthew. He was curious to learn what the white teacher was doing. Beck read to him the story of the cross. The savage and his companions listened with tearful eyes. "Tell me that again," exclaimed Kayarnak. He became at once a keen and earnest inquirer. He came and settled near the mission, bringing two other families, who became inquirers. The other South Greenlanders mocked and soon left; but five candidates for baptism, including Kayarnak, came out of the three families. Morning and evening prayers were established in these households, and they progressed rapidly in the knowledge of the Christian faith.

Sunday, March 29, 1739, was a great day at Herrnhut. Kayarnak, his wife, a son and a daughter, were baptized in the midst of prayers, thanksgivings, tears, and the melting power of the Spirit. The aged Egede had been called home by his king to teach the Esquimo language to those purposing to join the colony. But his son had taken his place in the mission-work, and rejoiced at this harvest home.

This baptism of the Spirit was followed by a baptism of blood. A brother of Kayarnak, who had become an inquirer, was killed, and Kayarnak himself was driven, with his family, under the threat of death, to South Greenland. But he carried the presence of the Saviour and the good news of salvation with him. Soon twenty-one boats, filled with his countrymen, came to Herrnhut inquiring about this new way and a risen Christ. At the expiration of a year Kayarnak himself, with his family, accompanied by a brother and family as inquirers, made their welcome appearance at the mission. After a brief but faithful career Kayarnak died, attesting joyfully in death, as he had in life, the power of Divine grace. The good work spread. In one Esquimo hut the inmates sat up all night listening with unwearied attention to the Word of Life.

In 1747 the material for a house of worship

was sent from Denmark by the friends of the mission, and it was dedicated with great joy. The next year thirty-five natives professed to obtain renewing grace and were baptized. A few years after a devastating disease was introduced from the whale-ships, and nearly two score of the native converts died; but in death they triumphed, and witnessed a good confession.

A few years later Matthew Stach, assisted by two recruits from the home congregation, established a new mission at a more southern point, which he called Lichtenfels. In a great emergency for a church, these brethren laid their case before God in prayer. God had given them the ears of the natives, whole families had professed to find Christ, and a house of worship was deemed necessary for the permanent usefulness of the mission. Thus situated, the winds and the strong current which had visited more southern shores brought a large amount of drift timber. Out of this the church was erected.

From this time the good work went steadily forward, its harvest-fields covering a greater area, its sowers and reapers increasing, and its sheaves more perfectly ripening for the heavenly garner. The whole New Testament was in due time translated and printed in Esquimo by the British and Foreign Bible Society. A training-school has been established at the Herrnhut Mission to prepare native Christians to preach to their countrymen. Re-union meetings of the native converts are at times held. At one of these two hundred and thirty-seven partook of the sacrament together, rejoicing with great joy.

Thus have arctic explorations been followed by the precious influences of the Gospel.

The reader will now readily recall the last chapter—its story of shipwreck and escape—and go with us on another voyage of exploration.

CHAPTER VIII.

A SUDDEN RETREAT.

THESE repeated disasters of the explorers seem not to have dampened the ardor of either the governments or the sailors in their desire to sail round the continents through the northern sea. Their desire to visit the North Pole was as intense as if they knew it to consist of a mountain of gold.

In 1743 the British Parliament offered a reward of one hundred thousand dollars to the lucky navigator who, sailing through Hudson Strait, should come out on the other side of the American continent. It appears to have been assumed that this prize could be taken by one giving certain proof that this *could be done.* So land as well as sea expeditions were tried. These started from the trading depots of the Hudson Bay Company, and traversed their vast territory toward the Arctic Sea. In 1869–72 Hearne reached a large and rapid river—the Coppermine—and floated nearly to its mouth. The next expedition, ten years later, by Mackenzie, followed the nobler Mackenzie River in the same direction. Neither were certain that they had reached the ocean. So the century closed with the vexed question unanswered.

Wars now for many years kept the thoughts and ships of commercial nations at home. Napoleon Bonaparte, fiercer than a polar bear, was making sad havoc of thrones. When, at last, the smoke of battles had cleared away, the attention to arctic exploration was renewed, largely by the influence of William Scoresby, a captain of a whale-ship. When a boy, in a whaler commanded by his father, he had reached a higher latitude than any yet attained. He was only twenty-one years old when his father retired from the service, giving his son the command of his ship.

In 1817 Captain Scoresby observed a remarkable change in the northern ice-fields. He reported that Baffin Bay, and the waters even far beyond, were free from ice, while large quantities were drifting south over the Atlantic to melt in a warmer region. He called the attention of Sir Joseph Banks, President of the Royal Society, to this remarkable fact in a well-written letter. The old enthusiasm began to glow among the great men. Scoresby's suggestions were readily taken up, but not the man. Though eminently qualified for the command, which he sought, of one of the exploring ships, only officers from the navy were allowed the honor, "red tape" prevailing over common sense and the best interests of exploration.

Two fine ships were soon in readiness: the larger, the "Isabella," three hundred and eighty-five tons, was commanded by Mr. (afterward Sir John) Ross; the smaller, the "Alexander," two hundred and fifty tons, was under the command of Lieutenant Edward Parry. These vessels were not only larger than their predecessors in the same service, but were better furnished in all respects. The best instruments known to science were on board, and a man skilled in using them, Captain Sabine, was detailed for that purpose. Not the least valuable member of this expedition was an Esquimo by the name of Sackhouse. He had been converted through the influence of the Danish mission in Greenland, and had been twice in Scotland, spending a considerable time under English instructors. He had a pleasing address and a true Christian spirit. He now joined the expedition as an interpreter.

A skillful draughtsman, Lieut. Hoppner, was taken to sketch the headlands and bays and other objects of interest, and to devote his time especially to laying down charts of the coast. Special stress was laid, in the orders given to Captain Ross, on the importance of affording the scientific officer and the artist every possible opportunity to operate in their departments of the service.

On the 30th of April, 1818, the ships sailed. Having passed the southern cape of Greenland, and coasting northernly, they were soon ice-locked. On one occasion the two ships made fast to an iceberg, and made a merry time of it. The officers admired the scenery. Far to the east was the dark outline of "Greenland's icy mountains," while to the west was a dreary horizon of masses of packed ice. For a short distance around their berg was open water.

Upon the berg itself were sights worth seeing. The scientific men—a little group—occupied an isolated spot, busy with their instruments. At a distant point a party of sailors were shooting sea-fowl, bringing down many at every shot; near the ship were sailors taking in ice for water; higher up the crystal mountain were some of the men amusing themselves by sliding down from the top into the valley below; others were quietly looking on, finding a real pleasure in seeing the happiness of their comrades. But the most exciting scene was a battle going on between a part of the officers and men of the two ships. High up the berg was a company behind an icy rampart. Below was an assailing party, boldly ascending, as best they could, the slippery height to dislodge them. Both parties were well armed—with snow-balls! The fight finally proved rather a *cold* one, and ended without bloodshed. It afforded a pleasant evidence that there were no jealousies among the members of this expedition.

Leaving the iceberg, they found favorable sailing until they reached the Danish and Esquimo settlement of Disco. Here was a fleet of twenty-five or thirty English whale-ships, waiting for the ice to open. It had the appearance of a home seaport.

A party of Esquimo came on board Captain Ross' ship, and the value of Sackhouse as an interpreter was soon seen. A trade for dogs and sledges was soon completed; after which the artist made a sketch of the group of natives, which greatly pleased them; they then danced Scotch reels on deck with the sailors, to the delight of all parties.

Sackhouse was especially attracted by one of the half-Danish young ladies. One of the officers, noticing his partiality, gave him a lady's shawl, sparkling with a spangled border, as a present to the young belle. He received it gladly, and presented it to her with a graceful bow. The young woman blushingly acknowledged the gift, and in return gave Sackhouse a pewter ring taken from her finger.

Sackhouse went on shore with the visitors, and not returning seasonably the next day, messengers were sent to hunt him up. He was found, after some search, in a hut seriously injured and suffering greatly. He had gone out early to shoot some specimens of natural history for the members of the scientific corps. Thinking, as he said, "Plenty powder, plenty kill," he had overloaded his gun. The result was "plenty hurt" in the breaking of his collar-bone by the recoil of his gun. It was a considerable time before his full recovery.

The ice breaking up, our explorers sailed, in company with the whalers, up the eastern side of Baffin Bay. While the whole fleet were within sight, at various distances, there occurred a natural phenomenon, curious enough to them, but quite common in the arctic regions. Some of these ships, by unequal refraction, appeared from the deck of the "Isabella" as if they were lifted up to a great height, while others at a greater distance were flattened to the surface of the sea.

The ships were soon taught to keep out of each other's way, as the mighty ice-currents sometimes brought them in violent collision with each other.

Occasionally the ships were towed along the edge of great masses of floating ice by the sailors tugging at a long rope. As the ice was thin, they not unfrequently broke through and received a cold bath. But as they did not happen all to break through at the same time, the unfortunate one had only to hold fast to the rope and be drawn out.

The explorers came, at one time, to an island about which were some Esquimo with their dog-sledges, the ice being unbroken on the land side. They had evidently never seen white men nor their ships. They looked amazed for awhile, and then scampered off. In a few hours they shyly returned. Sackhouse approached them with signs of peace. When at a distance he shouted, "Come on!" to which they replied, "No; go away!" One drew his knife, and added, "I can kill you!"

But Sackhouse was full of tact and courage. He threw them some beads and a shirt. These desirable things not quite overcoming their fears, he tossed them an English knife. They made a rush for this, and, as one picked it up, they all pulled their noses and exclaimed, "Heigh yaw!" Sackhouse pulled his own nose and echoed, "Heigh yaw!"

The gifts, nose pulling, and "yaws" were potent peace-makers, and a talk commenced.

"What," asked the natives, pointing to the ships, "are those great creatures?"

"Houses made of wood," said Sackhouse.

"No; they are alive. We saw them move their wings. Did they come from the sun or moon?"

"From that way," said Sackhouse, pointing south.

"No," said the doubting natives; "there is only ice that way."

As the Esquimo could not be enticed on board the ships, commanders Ross and Parry came out with their hands full of presents. The Esquimo began to move off at their approach. Sackhouse called to the officers to pull their noses and shout, "Heigh yaw!" The magic words opened a friendly intercourse. Among other gifts they were presented with a looking-glass. They gazed steadily at their own faces for a few moments in blank amazement, and then broke into an immoderate laugh, in which both parties joined heartily.

The expedition reached at last Smith Sound, as it was called, but Ross strangely passed it by without attempting an exploration; in the same way he passed Jones Sound, losing the opportunity of proving that they were both straits.

Entering Lancaster Sound, they found the water entirely free from ice in a westerly direction. With high hopes, before favoring winds, they sailed for awhile directly on the highway to the spice islands of India, as most, if not all the men, except Ross, believed. All at once the "Isabella" tacked ship on the return voyage. Parry reluctantly followed in the "Alexander," mortified and vexed. The expedition arrived safely in England, where a hue and cry was raised against Ross. He declared, in self-defense, that he clearly saw a-head a dark outline of mountain barriers, proving that navigation extended no further. As it has since been proved that none existed, it is not strange that Parry did not see them.

Thus ingloriously ended this finely-equipped expedition.

CHAPTER IX.

STRIKING INCIDENTS.

AT the same time that the Ross and Parry expedition left England for Baffin Bay, two other ships sailed on the same general errand. They were the "Dorothea" and "Trent." The first was commanded by Captain Buchan, in command also of the expedition, and the other by Lieutenant John Franklin. Captain Buchan was instructed to sail his ships between Spitzbergen and Greenland, touching at neither, but keeping straight on to the North Pole, and from thence to the appointed place of meeting with Ross' ships on the western coast of America. Both expeditions were to "conquer success," and *do* what others had so long *tried* to do. We have seen how Ross came out; let us follow Buchan.

He, too, as an incidental but important duty, was to see that all possible experiments were made during the voyage "on the elliptical figure of the earth; on magnetic phenomena; on the refraction of the atmosphere in high latitudes in ordinary circumstances, and over extensive masses of ice; and on the temperature and specific gravity of the sea at the surface and at various depths; and on meteorological and other interesting phenomena."

The two ships, having left England in April, 1818,

were in a few weeks entangled in the ice, with a storm upon them. They, however, kept together, and succeeded in getting under the lee of Bear Island, lying nearly two degrees south of Spitzbergen. This was then a famous fishing-ground, but was especially noted as a resort for walruses. The Muscovy Company sent its ships here for their oil. One ship's crew sometimes killed a thousand of these sea-monsters in a single day. Some of them are as large as the average size of our oxen. Their face is said to have somewhat of a human expression. It will appear from the following facts, given by Lieutenant Beechey, an officer of the expedition, that they possessed great affection among themselves, though savage toward their enemies. He says: "In the vast sheets of ice which surrounded the ships there were occasionally many pools; and when the weather was clear and warm, animals of various kinds would frequently rise and sport in them, or crawl from thence upon the ice to bask in the warmth of the sun. A walrus rose in one of these pools, or openings in the ice, close to the ship, and, finding every thing quiet, dived down and brought up its young, which it held by the breast by pressing it with its flipper. In this manner it moved about the pool, keeping in an erect posture, and always directing the face of the young toward the vessel. On the slightest movement on board the mother released her flipper and pushed the young one under the water; but when every thing was again quiet brought it up as before, and for a length of time continued to play about in the pool, to the great amusement of the seamen, who gave her credit for abilities in instructing her young, which, though possessed of considerable sagacity, she hardly merited."

Another scene presented by the walruses was quite as serious as amusing, and, though a little comic, came quite near being tragical. One of the sailors of the "Trent" having, from the ship's deck, wounded a walrus, a party of seamen manned a boat to secure the prize. No sooner had they pushed off from the ship than a detachment of the walrus army attacked them. They came on, snorting with rage, and terrific in numbers, size, and swiftness, with which they rushed to the assault. The boat's crew were taken by surprise and thrown off their guard. Some of the enemy, making a battering-ram of their heads, rushed furiously at the boat's sides, making it tremble in every joint with the concussion. Others endeavored to upset it by hanging over its sides while hooked on by their tusks. But the crew, recovering their self-possession, fought for their lives. They pricked the enemy in the face with sharp lances, or smote them over the head with hatchets. They, however, were growing faint with the unequal contest, while the walrus leaders pushed forward fresh recruits to take the place of their wounded comrades. Just at this crisis a monster walrus, evidently the champion assailant, rushed upon the boat and seized it with his great tusks. He had darted in, to end the fray, proclaim the victory, and carry off the spoils. But there was one loaded gun in the boat which had been held in reserve, as there was no time to load others. This a sailor seized, thrust its muzzle down the monster's throat, and fired. The boastful champion floated off, a lifeless mass of oil and blubber. His companions instantly snorted a retreat, and literally bore him off, keeping him from sinking by swimming under him, and bearing him up by their tusks.

At one time a large number of walruses were basking in the sun upon the beach. The seamen fired into them, wounding several, while the rest rushed into the sea. Recovering from their panic, they returned, and seeing no enemy near commenced tumbling their wounded fellows over with their tusks until they reached the water; thus recovering the fallen, they all disappeared together.

On the 28th of May an arctic fog enveloped the ships soon after they had sailed for Bear Island. A blinding snow was added to the fog, and the ships lost sight of each other. They had agreed that in such a case they would meet in Magdalena Bay, a good anchorage on the north-west side of Spitzbergen, where they were both snugly sheltered on the 3d of June. They had learned, as might have been expected, that it was impossible to sail to the pole, as they had been instructed, without touching either at Greenland or Spitzbergen. "That little way to the North Pole," as one of their patrons had lightly termed it, was a bit harder to navigate than the landsman supposed.

A marked feature of Magdalena Bay was four glaciers, the smallest two hundred feet high, moving seaward over the slope of a mountain. The largest of the four extended several miles inland; the smallest was called the "Hanging Iceberg," as it seemed ready at any time to drop into the sea. So slightly, in fact, did the projecting ice of the glaciers adhere to the mountain or the congealed mass behind it, that the least noise brought down a berg. Beechey describes two very grand launches of this kind, which the explorers were fortunate enough to witness. He says: "The first was occasioned by the discharge of a musket at about a half a mile's distance from the glacier. Immediately after the report of the gun a noise like thunder was heard in the direction of the glacier, and in a few seconds more an immense piece broke away and fell headlong into the sea. The crew of the launch, supposing themselves to be beyond its influence, quietly looked upon the scene. Presently a sea arose and rolled toward the shore with such rapidity, that the crew had no time to take any precautions. The boat was in consequence washed upon the beach and completely filled by the succeeding wave. As soon as their astonishment had subsided they examined their boat. They found her so badly stove that it was necessary to repair her in order to return to the ship. They had also the curiosity to measure the distance the boat had been carried by the wave, and found it to be ninety-six feet."

At another time Beechey and his companions were treated to a still grander sight: "This occurred," he says, "on a remarkably fine day, when the quietness of the bay was first interrupted by the falling body. Lieutenant Franklin and myself had approached one of these stupendous walls of ice, and were endeavoring to search into the innermost recess of a deep cavern that was near the foot of the glacier, when we heard a report as of a cannon, and, turning to the quarter whence it proceeded, we perceived an immense piece of the point of the berg sliding down from the height of two hundred feet at least, into the sea. It dispersed the water in every direction, accompanied by a loud grinding noise. A quantity of water which had previously been lodged in fissures, now made its escape over the point of the glacier, in many small cataracts."

The immense waves created by this majestic launch, rolled over the bay and struck the "Dorothea," which lay upon her side, aground, four miles away. They released her tackle, put her in an upright position, and passed on, seeming to laugh at the sport they made as she reeled and tumbled at their bidding. Beechey adds: "The piece that had been disengaged, at first wholly disappeared under water, and nothing was seen but a violent boiling of the sea, and a shooting up of clouds of spray, like that which occurs at the foot of a great cataract. After a time it reappeared, raising its head full a hundred feet above the surface, with water pouring down from all parts of it. Then, laboring as if in doubt which way it should fall, it rolled over, and, after rocking about some minutes, at length became settled. We now approached and found it nearly a quarter of a mile in circumference, and sixty feet out of water. Knowing its specific gravity, and making a fair allowance for its inequalities, we computed its weight at 451,660 tons. A stream of salt water was still flowing down its sides, and there was a continual cracking noise, as loud as that of a cart whip, occasioned, I suppose, by the escape of confined air."

Our explorers found, as others have done, the temperature on the west coast of Spitzbergen to be mild, there being little sensation of cold, even when the thermometer was only a few degrees above freezing. When the sun shone through the pure atmosphere the effect was enlivening and brilliant. The azure hue was more clearly defined than that of an Italian sky. The radiation of the sun was intense at times. Beechey says: "Hence are found rarities of Alpine plants, grasses, and lichens, such as in more southern climes flourish in great luxuriance. They are found ascending to a considerable height, so that we have frequently seen the raindeer browsing at an elevation of fifteen hundred feet."

The shores of the islands of Spitzbergen are the resort of animals of various kinds and in great numbers. The explorers found Magdalena Bay a lively place in this respect. Sea birds, of various species, filled the air with their merry cries. Wherever they went, groups of walruses were basking in the sun and indulging in their playful roar. The husky bark of the seal saluted their ears by day and night.

Beechey in referring to the great numbers of "the little auk," one variety of sea-fowl, says: "We have frequently seen an uninterrupted line of them, extending full half way over the bay, or to a distance of more than three miles, and so close together that thirty have fallen at one shot. This living column might be about six yards broad and as many deep; so that, allowing six birds to a cubic yard, there would be four millions of these creatures on the wing at one time. They rise in such numbers as to darken the air, and their chorus is distinctly audible at a distance of four miles."

At one of the islets they found the Eider-duck in such numbers that it was difficult to walk without treading on their nests. Against all ordinary intruders of the sea-fowl kind they fought with courage. When foxes, or other larger animals, approached, they hastily drew over their eggs the down of their nests and glued it down by an offensive yellow fluid. This protection was complete when once the enemy snuffed the odor.

The islands near the anchorage of the ships were clothed with a soft carpet of moss. To these pastures herds of deer swam, feasted, and grew fat in great numbers. One small island above supplied the expedition with forty carcasses, the fat on the loins of which was from four to six inches thick. One of them weighed two hundred and eighty-five pounds.

Of the affection of these beautiful animals Beechey thus writes: "They showed evident marks of affection for each other. They were at this time in pairs, and when one was shot the other would hang over it and occasionally lick it, bemoaning its fate; and, if not immediately killed, would stand three or four shots rather than leave its companion. This compassionate conduct, it is needless to say, doubled our chance of success, though I must confess it was obtained in violation of our better feelings."

The boats of the "Trent" captured several reindeer as they were swimming from one island to another. These they attempted to domesticate on board of the ship, but the poor things were so frightened that they broke their limbs in their struggles, and were in mercy killed.

On the 7th of June the ships attempted to proceed on their voyage to the pole. They had the usual amount of buffetings by the winds, driftings by adverse currents, and collisions and impediments in the floating ice, resulting in their return, after about three weeks, to Magdalena Bay.

Resting awhile, and repairing damages, they again steered northward. This time the ship "Dorothea" was more roughly handled, and came near going down with all her crew. The "Trent," under the management of the skillful Franklin, fared better, but was badly battered. Both returned to Spitzbergen for repairs, and then reluctantly returned to England with the old report —Ice is king at the north!

CHAPTER X.

IMPORTANT SUCCESS.

THE two explorations just noticed—Ross' to Lancaster Sound, and Buchan's to Spitzbergen—having ended, others were immediately projected. Commander Ross fell into the back ground for seeing mountain obstacles where none were. His second in command, Lieutenant Parry, was the "coming man." He had declared that all attempts at the north had been abandoned on the eve of success. His faith and courage were suited to the spirit of the times, and his subsequent success proved that both sprung from real strength of character. As we are to sail with this noted discoverer now for the first time in full command, let us pause and seek a more intimate acquaintance before we start.

Edward Parry was the son of Dr. Parry, of Bath, England. He early manifested a desire to see the world. When a child he was once found in his father's library astride of a globe. Not finding it the most convenient hobby-horse, he looked on this side and then on that, as he sat mounted, and exclaimed, "How wise it would be to go round it!" Yet he neither purposed nor desired to enter the navy. But a divinity directed the tide of his life, which he wisely took at the flood. Until within a few days of his first sea voyage he was studying his father's profession, which he intended soon to enter. It happened that just at this time a lady friend was visiting the family who was related to Admiral Cornwallis, then in command of the Channel Fleet. With a woman's instinct, this lady friend had seen Edward's adaptation to the sea, and had often urged his father to place him in the navy. Strange enough, she at this moment succeeded, when he was on the eve of professional life—the father consenting and the son agreeing to go on a sea voyage. Admiral Cornwallis was "interviewed," and in a few days Edward was shipped on board the "Ville de Paris." His ship was immediately sent to aid in blockading the French coast to prevent Bonaparte from invading England. He afterward saw service in the Baltic, and later, in the arctic seas, with the whale-fishery protection fleet. He had been in Halifax almost soon enough to snuff the smoke of the famous battle between the "Chesapeake" and "Shannon." So, though he had not gone round the globe, he had peered over some of its edges. In 1817 he was recalled from service in Bermuda by the alarming illness of his father. Remaining idle for some time he felt a sailor's restlessness, and wrote to a friend, seeking a position in an *African* discovery expedition. Before closing the letter, his eye fell upon a scrap in a newspaper concerning a *polar* expedition. He at once added: "Hot or cold is all one to me —Africa or the Pole." This letter was shown to

Mr. Barrow—Secretary of the Admiralty, afterward Sir John—then the chief official promoter of arctic discovery voyages. He smiled, pocketed the letter, and obtained for Edward a commission as second in command of the John Ross expedition, where we have made a slight but favorable acquaintance with him.

Let us now return to the story of this chapter—Parry's first voyage in full command.

In two months after the arrival in England of the ships sent out in 1818, two ships, the "Hecla" and "Griper," were sent into the naval dock to be made as strong as oak and iron could be made, to fight the arctic ice in the spring of 1819. Great deliberation and careful inquiry and examination were used by the Admiralty before selecting a commander. But Parry said playfully, "I am sure they will give me some finger in this new pie." He was at last put in command, and given the authority necessary to equip the ships and appoint their officers and crew. The command of the "Griper," a gun-brig of one hundred and eighty tons, was given to Lieutenant Liddon.

It is a singular fact that while Parry was given this flattering authority, yet he sailed on this expedition with no higher rank than that of lieutenant, while his neglected former commander, Ross, was promoted to a captaincy. The promotion was given, probably, to conciliate wounded pride. Parry, who never seemed at a loss for a pertinent word, complacently remarks in reference to these facts: "Promotion is nothing to the command of the 'Hecla,' with the chart of Lancaster Sound in my hand."

The two vessels contained ninety-four men, fifty-eight in the "Hecla," and thirty-six in the "Griper." They sailed on the 11th of May, 1819, a fortnight later than the start of the preceding year. But they made better time by a month in reaching the mouth of Lancaster Sound. But to reach it they had to fight their way along the west coast of Greenland, although they had no worse difficulty than "floes" and threatening bergs. But when they undertook to force their way through the middle pack, the work was truly terrifying. Now they were pushing cautiously through the loose current or wind-driven ice; then they were "tracking" along the edge of ice as solid, apparently, as the land, the sailors strung along with the drag ropes over their shoulders; and, at another time, they hastily "tumbled" into their boats to tow the ship from a threatened "nip" between two icebergs. A week was thus spent; the western side of Baffin Bay was gained. With a fair, fresh breeze, a clear sea and jubilant feelings, the ships entered, and went spanking up Lancaster Sound. The mast-heads were crowded by the officers, and the men were scattered about the rigging, all with throbbing hearts, waiting the developments of their sailing through these hitherto unknown waters. The men on deck received the messages sent down from the crow's-nest with almost breathless interest. Every day's western progress added to their now greatly excited hope. On and still on they sailed, and no bugbear mountains impeded their course, nor for a long time did any real obstacle destroy their cherished expectations. Once land ahead caused a momentary despondency, but it proved to be an island. In endeavoring to go south of it, they discovered an opening from the Sound southward which Parry named Prince Regent Inlet. Soon after they discovered a broad channel to the north, and called it Wellington Channel. Thus they were giving to the world a knowledge of these important waters which stand so prominent on the present maps of the arctic regions.

When they had sailed to the 100° west longitude, a curious and important incident occurred. The compasses first became very sluggish, and then failed altogether as they turned into Prince Regent Inlet. They felt sure the "magnetic north pole" was not far away, but they could not stop to ascertain the interesting fact, for were they not at last on the long-sought northern highway to India? What was the magnetic pole to that? They soon reached the meridian, 110° west from Greenwich. His majesty's government had offered $25,000 to those of his subjects who first reached this point, and the money was now theirs! They lay now off a large island to which they gave the name Melville. They pushed on some days more, slowly and laboriously towing and warping the ships, until they were reluctantly convinced that nothing was left to them but to find, as well as they could, the best harbor in which to spend

Sawing a Channel.

the long arctic winter. On the 12th of September they were held fast by the ice. A company was sent out to obtain information concerning their position, and they were overtaken by a snow-storm, and did not return at the appointed time. Four other parties were sent in search of them, and several days of painful suspense passed before all were safely returned. A good harbor was found, under Melville Island, two miles off. To this they resolved to cut a channel and track their ships. They accomplished it in four days, officers and men working in good spirits, though often up to their knees in water. They anchored the ships about a "cable's length" from the shore, amid the heartiest cheers.

Parry's qualifications as a leader in an arctic adventure were now more than ever to be tested. To govern men having the sharp points of character possessed by sailors requires a master-hand, even when there is work for them to do, and hope of the immediate accomplishment of a desired end to stimulate them. But to keep them under discipline and in good spirits through long months of darkness, with nothing to do, is the test of superior tact and energy. Fortunately Parry was equal to the situation.

The ships were immediately stripped of their sails, the upper decks cleared and covered in. This made a roomy place for exercise and amusements. Hunting parties were organized and "game laws" established, that they who "stayed by the stuff" might share with those who took the prey.

But game was not abundant. The musk-ox's time to arrive at the vicinity was in May, and his time to leave was the last of September—just as the strangers arrived. Bears were occasional visitors, and the deer herds remained only through October. The men seemed not to be skilled in taking these animals, though they shot a few deer. Once a bear followed a man to the very side of the ship. He was wounded, but got off. On another occasion fifteen deer were seen lying down, not afar off, guarded by a faithful stag, who stood as a sentinel with head and ears erect. They were approached by the hunters and off they ran, their leader giving the alarm and occasionally making the entire circuit of the fleeing herd as if to warn them to keep together; when any one lagged behind he quickened its steps by a blow on the rump with his horns. Not one was taken by the pursuers. Neither seals nor walruses were seen; even most of the sea-fowls left before mid-winter. Wolves and foxes remained to give hideousness to the darkness. The "great whales" were abundant, but none accommodatingly stranded upon the beach, as they did for the shipwrecked islanders of the Bering expedition.

Vegetation was as meager as the animals were few. Dwarfed willows, a mean saxifrage, and small mosses and grass, made nearly the sum of Melville Island greenness. It was, indeed, a dismal place, and contrasted sharply with the hoped-for islands beyond the continent to which they believed, a few weeks before, they were sailing,

But Parry kept the thoughts of his men pleasantly occupied.

Each day all took a dose of lime-juice and water as a preventive of scurvy. The sailors had their times of marching around the cleared and covered upper-deck, to the tune of a hand-organ and vivacious songs.

The sun left them the 5th of November, but the men's thoughts were taken from the gloomy fact by the commencement of a series of ingeniously continued amusements. Dramatical performances had been suggested, and Lieutenant Beechey was appointed manager; other officers came forward as "star" performers. The plays were both original and selected, Parry writing some of them himself. The preparations, of course, excited the curiosity of the sailors, and gave them pleasant anticipations; and when the first performance, that of "Miss in her Teens," came off, they were convulsed with laughter, and were supplied with a topic of talk for their idle hours.

Another means of diversion was the publishing of a weekly newspaper. Parry had given the name of North Georgian to certain islands of the vicinity, so the paper was called, "The North Georgian Gazette and Winter Chronicle." All were invited to contribute, Captain Sabine taking charge as editor. Doubtless its pages were very spicy, and its weekly appearance looked for with interest; but the lack of a column of "home news" was sadly missed.

When Christmas came it was enlivened by a

dramatic performance of "The North-west Passage," written by Parry. All had as good a dinner as the circumstances allowed. The officers' table was supplied with a piece of English roast beef, preserved since May without salt, simply by freezing.

The sun reappeared above the horizon the 7th of February. On the 17th of March daylight had so far ventured as to invite all to outside work, so the dramatic performance closed with a spirited and appropriate address.

Parry now improved the time in making explorations. They found on the western side "one of the most habitable and pleasantest spots yet seen in the arctic regions, the vegetation being more abundant than in any other place, and the situation favorable for game."

The ships were not released from their icy fetters until the 1st of August. Before they left, a large block of sandstone was selected on which they engraved a record of their stay.

When relieved from their ten months' imprisonment the explorers made perilous efforts to sail farther west. But on the 26th of August, after a consultation of the officers of both ships, a voyage home by the old way was declared to be the only sensible course to be pursued.

They arrived in England in two months, and were received joyfully; and well they might be, for Parry had greatly enlarged the knowledge of the polar regions, and made a long stride toward the western opening of the north-west passage. He had, too, brought back every man with whom he sailed, excepting one seaman, who died at Melville Island of an old disease.

Parry was immediately promoted to the rank of commander, and honors were showered upon him from every quarter. But as for himself, his first act on landing was to march, at the head of his officers and men, to church, to render public thanksgiving to God for their preservation, and to acknowledge his hand in their success.

CHAPTER XI.

ARCTIC SEA-MONSTERS.

OUR narrative of arctic discovery thus far has shown that the vast extent of waters included in Davis Strait and Baffin Bay had become considerably well-known to the civilized world. But the reader may be disposed to inquire, What profit to mankind have been these perilous adventures? We shall not be surprised if this question is frequently asked as we proceed. Since the question is a natural and proper one, we will pause occasionally to answer it as far as we are able.

The Greenland whale-fishery followed in the wake of these discoveries, and has, down to a late period, been a source of wealth both to the new and old world. It is so *arctic* in its character that our knowledge of this icy region would be imperfect without a sketch of this perilous business. Fortunately we have the material for such a sketch furnished by William Scoresby, brought before the reader on a previous page, a captain of a whale-ship, an intelligent man, a bold explorer of the early part of this century, and a true Christian.

The old Northmen did a little at catching the monsters of the deep in the waters north-east of

Greenland. In the history of Ohther's voyages, in the tenth century, there is something said about the Norwegian whalemen. They carried on this great business on a small scale, no doubt, and with little capital. Later accounts speak of whales on the shores of France and Spain, troubling the nets of the fishermen. As the whales scorned the nets, which, indeed, were not set for them, the fishermen shot their arrows into their huge bodies. These, very likely, were at first scorned, too; but men are always great on expedients to conquer inferior animals, so that his majesty of the sea became, in time, subjected to the lord of creation.

Whales, like ships, have in every age been occasionally wrecked. This comes not from being blown ashore, nor, we presume, from being carried ashore by strong currents, but by pursuing their prey too eagerly toward the beaches, and so getting aground. It may be that they get up exploring expeditions, and are too eager to see the men and things on land, just as men are often wrecked by being too eager to see the whales and other sights on the sea. Be that as it may, so common was it in 1315 for whales to get stranded on the British Islands that the king, Edward II., declared by law that "all wrecked whales shall belong to the crown," and a hundred years later Henry IV. gave to the Bishop of Rochester all the stranded whales on the coast of his bishopric. What this "picking" amounted to we are not informed, but it must have been regarded by the bishop as rather a fishy way of supporting his dignity.

The ships of the Russian Company were the first "to strike oil" in the west Greenland seas. This was in 1611, and the next year all maritime Europe was attacked by the oil fever, and fleets spread all sail for these waters. The whales here caught were not as large as those they had been catching, as they seldom exceeded sixty-five feet long, whereas those mostly caught near Spitzbergen were not seldom a hundred feet. But these are a different species, having no fins along their backs—"smooth backs," as the sailors call them—and they contain a wonderfully large fountain of oil. Their head is immense; and the lip, which is from fifteen to twenty feet in breadth, and five to six in height, is attached to the underjaw, and forms the cavity of the mouth. This, when open, must therefore expose a very roomy place—a comfortable sitting-room, at least, for a small family. Scoresby thinks that such a mouth would contain a ship's "jolly-boat," "men and all." Parts of such boats, with now and then a man, have certainly been taken into such mouths in the deadly conflicts between these whales and the whalers. In these cases the *boat* may be "jolly," but the *men* are in another state of mind altogether.

The fins, placed about a third of the length of the body from the snout, are from seven to nine feet long, and four or five feet broad. Immense paddles are these, when worked by an engine sixty feet long! The tail of the whale is an article he much esteems, and, if consulted whether to part with his head or tail, would, we are sure, unhesitatingly say, "Neither!" It contains a hundred square feet, supposing it to belong to one of average size, and it is with this, in part, that he tries to escape from his enemies, the whalemen; not succeeding in this, or if taken unawares, he frightens them off by a commotion with it which makes the sea boil; or he may give it a flourish and send boat and men high in the air, or to take their last plunge in the great deep.

His eyes, placed in the side of his head, are small—only about the size of those of the ox. He has no ears, and no place can be discovered for the admission of sound until the skin is removed. So he is slow to hear, quick to see, and great at blowing. The way the latter is done is this: he has on the top of his head two nostrils, that is, holes, narrow, but six or eight inches long. Through these the whale breathes, throwing high into the air, when he does so, a vapor mixed with mucous, making at the same time a loud noise.

This Greenland whale has a mouthful of whalebone, which answers his purpose instead of teeth. It is the same article that we have for umbrella-frames and other uses; but in the mouth of the original owner it is in wide, long sheets with a hair-like fringe. These sheets or plates are suspended from each side of the upper jaw. A large whale carries in this way a ton and a half of this article.

When feeding on the minute animals which crowd the olive-colored waters, the Greenland whale swims swiftly just under the surface, with his capacious mouth open. The water which thus pours into it goes out at its sides, passing through the hair-like strainer, leaving the food behind.

The female whale gives birth in the spring to one offspring, to which she gives nourishment at her breast. Her new-born child is a nice large baby, often fourteen feet long. It stays by its mother a year or more, and there is the strongest affection between them. Scoresby relates the following incident illustrative of this:—

"The men of a whale-ship's boat launched a harpoon into a baby whale, or 'sucker,' which was unwatchfully sporting in the deep with its mother. It was easily drawn to the stern of the boat by the line attached to the cruel harpoon which had entered the vitals of its victim. The mother, for the moment, had not missed her child. When she saw what had been done while she was off her guard, she came at the boat with a fury that made even the brave old whalemen tremble. Bending with all their might to their oars they rowed away from their maddened enemy, at the same time letting the line out to which was attached the young whale, which, of course, dropped far astern. The mother, though mad enough to swallow the boat, men and all, stopped, picked up her wounded child, and started off in an opposite direction. Six hundred feet of line were run out, making a heavy burden for her, in addition to the object of her care. When the end of the line was reached the men still retained its attachment to the boat, thus giving the whale the boat to carry as well as the line and the 'sucker.' Still she clung to it, darting this way and that to disengage it from the line. While her maternal affection was thus exhausting her, the boat stole up, harpoons were plunged into her, and mother and young became the prey of the fishermen."

The arctic whale, though it can fight for its young, and is dangerous when closely pressed, is very timid and unconscious of its strength. If it were not so the whalemen would fare badly. When struck by the harpoon, slyly thrown into him, he rounds up his back, turns his head downward, throws up his enormous tail, and dives down—down he goes at the rate of ten or twelve miles an hour, and stops not until he reaches bottom. The line attached to the harpoon he carries with him smokes as it runs over the side of the boat, and woe be to the man around whose legs it may accidentally be coiled; he is jerked overboard and carried down, or his limb torn from his body. The boat even, if the line "fouls," that is, fastens to any part of it, is carried under, like the cork on a boy's fishing-line when a big fish gets hold of the bait.

When the whale has been down from twenty to thirty minutes, up his huge form rises to the surface, disturbing the sea and rolling great waves over its surface. The watchful boats cautiously approach, and the monster receives sharp thrusts from steel-pointed lances, or from more deadly harpoons. The signal is given, and fresh crews and other boats hasten to the scene of conflict. The sea, and sometimes the men, are stained with blood. If there is an ice-floe near, the whale immediately rushes for it and dives beneath the surface. If the whalemen's line of a mile or two long runs out before the whale is out of breath, his tormentors are glad to "cut away" and lose line, whale, and all, rather than risk being drawn under the ice. If no such refuge is at hand the frightened, bleeding, exhausted monster continues to dive and rise to the surface, the whalemen all the while greeting his reappearance with a thrust of their weapons, now wounding, and then, with the shout of "Stern, all!" darting as swiftly away. It is brute strength against intelligent skill, and the contest is unequal. That tail does occasionally strike avenging blows which clothes a whole ship's company in mourning, and puts its flag at half mast when she returns home; but the sea-monster is loser in the conflict.

The following incidents will show the whale's side of the contest. A small whale was harpooned by a ship's boat. Other boats at the moment pushed off from the ship to share the danger and triumph of the fray. But the whale proved to be both wide awake and plucky. After his first dive he started off on the run. The relief boat came up, for, with a boat in tow, an iron in his side, and the exhaustion of a long, breathless dive, he made only slow time. The harpoons of four boats were lodged in him, but still he pushed ahead. One boat, thinking to end the chase, ventured too near, and was instantly sunk. Finally, he took in tow six miles of line and three boats, but he was not captured until he had drawn his captors nine miles from the ship.

At another time a boat made fast to a whale. By hard rowing two others attached themselves, and all pricked him with their sharp lances, and lacerated him with their harpoons at every opportunity. To get rid of these annoyances he struck off from east to south under water. Having obtained a mile of line he swung round in a circuit, working off at the same time from the ship. This serious sport went on for seven hours, and then a storm arose. But both sides refused to yield the contest. To impede the progress of the whale, and to keep together, the boats were lashed one to the other, and put broadside to. Still the smitten monster tugged away at the line, now weighing of itself half a ton, for another seven hours. The night being at hand and the storm increasing, the boats began to think of retreating. But to cover their retreat they attached the end of the line to a large cask, and moored one of the boats to the cask, raised upon it the ship's flag, and abandoned the whole. They lay by as near as possible during the night, and in the morning looked upon a deserted field. All was gone, and they returned ingloriously to the ship.

While some whales thus showed fight, the greater number yielded their coveted treasures of oil, and the arctic whalemen, while often adding quite as much as the mere explorers to the world's knowledge of the northern seas, enriched their owners.

One ship's cargo of whalebone and oil sometimes sold for a hundred thousand dollars.

But these gains, like the knowledge of the explorers, were obtained at the expense of much suffering from the cold, great risks from blinding fogs, from icebergs, ice-floes, currents, and storms, as well as of much peril from the whales themselves. The early whalers which followed in the wake of discovery ships seldom returned with all the men with whom they left home. Flags at half-mast, on returning to the home harbor, solemnly attested the dangers of hunting the arctic sea-monsters.

CHAPTER XII.

DOWN THE COPPERMINE.

IN our story of Buchan's expedition to the Spitzbergen waters we introduced, as second in command, John Franklin. Since he is now to appear chief actor in scenes of daring and peril, and is to be long before us in our narratives of the adventures of others, we give a few facts of his previous history. He was trained from boyhood for a life on the sea. He first appears in history as a midshipman on the Australian coast survey. While thus engaged he was shipwrecked in the "Porpoise." As midshipman and master's mate he was in the fleet with the naval hero, Nelson, and at the battle of Copenhagen. He was lieutenant at the bloody battle of Trafalgar, in 1805. He belonged to the ship "Bedford" in the attack on New Orleans in 1815, and there, commanding in the boats, he was wounded. His conduct on the occasion received "honorable notice" in the report of his superior officer. He obtained, in his naval experience, the reputation of a thorough seaman, a skillful surveyor, an apt handler of nautical instruments, and a high-minded, honorable man.

The spring after his return with the Buchan expedition he was given the independent command of a new one, at the same time that his friend Parry was so honored. But it was one somewhat out of the line of his previous experience. He was instructed to proceed through Hudson Bay to one of its designated depots on its coast, then to go by land to the source of the Coppermine River, follow it down to the Arctic Sea, and push his way in boats along the coast eastward. It was hoped that Parry and Franklin would thus meet and prove a north-west passage.

Franklin left England on this hazardous undertaking in May, 1819. His companions were John Richardson, naval surgeon, George Back and Robert Hood, midshipmen, and John Hepburn, servant. Dr. Richardson was an enthusiastic and competent naturalist. The midshipmen were apt sketchers of natural objects, and skillful in mapping out the surveys. The servant proved himself a worthy helper in the enterprise, and not inferior to any member of the expedition in times of great exigency.

They arrived at the York Factory, on the south-western shore of Hudson Bay, August 30, after full an average amount of arctic peril from the ice, currents, and storms of the bay. Here they were provided with a boat for river voyaging, provisions, ammunition, and such necessary things demanded by the enterprise. On the 9th of September they set out, and, after ascending numerous rivers, crossing lakes and swamps, making portages around falls, and weary climbing over hills, they arrived at Cumberland House, on Pine Lake, the latter part of October. They had traveled full seven hundred miles. The midshipmen had taken sketches. Dr. Richardson had secured valuable contributions to science, and their combined efforts had resulted in a survey of the route. Here they paused until January. They were now on a chain of lakes, including the Slave Lakes, which bore north-west, and then nearly due north, until, with contiguous rivers, they communicated with the source of the Coppermine. In January the party divided, and Franklin, Back, and Hepburn pushed north-west to Fort Chipeway, on Lake Athabaska, Dr. Richardson and Midshipman Hood remaining at the Cumberland House until spring. Franklin arrived at his point of destination the 26th of March, having made a journey of eight hundred and fifty-seven miles. The party complained bitterly of the difficulty of snow-shoe traveling. A clumsy machine of two or three pounds weight, attached to swollen ankles and galling, bleeding feet, kept them often in an agony of pain.

When the April rains thawed the ice, innumerable frogs commenced an incessant din. So instantaneous was their croak, with the loosening of the ice, that Mr. Hood declared that they must have come forth full grown, and just as the fall freezing arrested them. Franklin speaks of some experiments Dr. Richardson made of the effect of cold on fishes. Several were taken in a lively condition from the water and frozen in a low temperature for thirty-six hours. In this state they could be broken by a blow from the hatchet, and their intestines taken out solid. When exposed to warmth and gradually thawed, they were wide awake again and ready for a swim.

In July Dr. Richardson and Hood having joined the party, Franklin began to think of pushing forward. Sixteen Canadian half-breeds—French and Indian—were engaged to accompany them, to whose party a Chipeway woman was soon added. With these the expedition left the fort the latter part of July, 1820, in three boats, the crews joining as they paddled off in a lively boat song. At one of their early stopping-places they secured two interpreters, and the valuable services of a Mr. Wentzel, an agent of the fur company, who was to manage the Canadians of the expedition—no light task—and the Indians whom they might meet, he being experienced in both branches of service.

An Indian chief by the name of Akaitcho, and several of his men, joined them soon, and were useful as hunters. All went well for awhile, the discoverers making good progress northward. Deer were plenty, and the hunters were successful in getting a supply from their herds, and securing other game. But as they went north the deer disappeared, and their provisions were not abundant. The Canadians became discontented on short rations, and threatened rebellion. This feeling Franklin at once checked by stringent discipline. But the whole party were soon brought to a stand. They built huts, and went into winter-quarters, calling the place Fort Enterprise. They had traveled five hundred and fifty miles since leaving Fort Chipeway, making over fifteen hundred miles since the commencement of the year, and twenty-two hundred since leaving York Factory.

When established in his winter-quarters, Franklin planned a journey to the head-waters of the Coppermine. He declared his desire of assuming all the risk of an immediate descent to the sea, even, and inquired of the chief Akaitcho what he thought of it. "Well," he replied, after using all the argument occurring to him, "I have said every thing I can urge to dissuade you from going on this service, on which it seems you wish to sacrifice your lives as well as the Indians who might attend you; however, if after all I have said you are determined to go, some of my young men shall join the party, because it shall not be said that we permitted you to die alone, after having brought you hither; but from the moment they embark in the canoes, I and their relatives shall mourn them as dead."

Thus, no doubt, wisely counseled, Franklin gave up the idea of reaching the sea, but he sent off Hood and Back, with a few Canadians, in a canoe, to ascertain the distance to the Coppermine River, while he and Dr. Richardson started afoot for the same purpose. After much suffering from great exposures and insufficient food, both parties were glad to get back to Fort Enterprise.

It was soon apparent that Franklin's large party could not live on the resources of the vicinity, and have provisions enough for the voyage to the sea. In this emergency Back volunteered to return to Fort Chipeway and hurry along supplies, which were to come from the Cumberland House. This most daring proposition was accepted, and Mr. Wentzel, two Canadians, and two Indians, with their wives, agreed to go with him. This party set out October 18. Wentzel, on reaching Fort Providence, returned, taking two Esquimo guides with him. Back and the Canadians and Indians suffered greatly as they pushed forward. Being nearly starved, one of the women cut a hole in the ice and caught a fine pike, and gave it all to the white men, not one of the Indians being willing to eat a morsel of it. On being asked why, they replied: "There will not be enough for us all, and we are accustomed to starvation, but you are not."

At one time while crossing on the ice a narrow arm of Slave Lake he fell through. Though the cold was intense, he escaped unhurt. On another occasion while crossing a sheet of ice over deep water it began to give way; he increased his speed, the ice bending beneath his feet, and he had a long race for life, not daring to stop until he reached the shore. The party had no better lodging-place than a camp in the woods, and Back had for a covering only a blanket and deer skin, while the thermometer was often forty degrees below zero, and once fifty-seven below. Sometimes they were two or three days without any food, and not unfrequently on short allowance. We shall not wonder, then, at the following statement: "One of our men caught a fish one day, which with some moss scraped from a rock made us a tolerable supper. While we were eating it I perceived one of the women busily scraping an old skin, with the contents of which her husband presented us. This consisted of pounded meat and fat, but a greater proportion of Indian and deer hair than either. It was eaten by us, after three days' privation, as a great luxury."

It was under such circumstances that Back made the whole journey to Fort Chipeway and back on foot, much of the time on snow-shoes, traveling in all eleven hundred and four miles. He was absent five months, but returned safely, probably saving the expedition by bringing in timely supplies. No more heroic act is on record, nor one exhibiting greater power of physical endurance. Even the Indian women must have conceded that this white man could *starve* and walk with the best of the Indians. During the five months of Back's absence, the party at Fort Enterprise had no small fight with cold and hunger. Fish were caught until the fifth of November, and afforded a timely supply of food. After that they were sometimes short of necessary sustenance. The cold in the mean time froze the trees to their very centers. So hard were they that in attempting to cut them they spoiled their axes, so that by the end of December only one was fit to use. This embarrassed them in getting fuel for their fires.

The chief of his men were off much of the time on hunting excursions, while the people in the fort were anxiously waiting the result.

It is pleasant to state that, under these circumstances, the Sabbath was strictly kept as God's day, Divine service was regularly performed; the wood of the day was laid in on Saturday, and all secular labor, not a necessity, was omitted. The Canadians attended, though Roman Catholics; not understanding English perfectly, the Lord's Prayer and the Apostles' Creed were read to them in French.

Each day they had two cups of tea without sugar, and on Sunday they broke the monotony by taking one cup of chocolate instead.

Akaitcho had little success in hunting, and the number of his followers who hung about the fort expecting to be fed had increased to forty; he was at last persuaded to take them and leave. He insisted, however, on leaving behind, to be supported by the discoverers, several women, among whom was his wife and daughter. The daughter, Green Stocking, was esteemed very beautiful, and had been twice married, though only sixteen years old. Her mother now wished her to remain with her, and so she was quite annoyed when Mr. Hood took her portrait, for she said:—

"The Great Chief of the pale faces may send and take her to be his wife."

Various expedients were devised to occupy the minds of the party in the long ten months' imprisonment. The officers were, of course, much employed with their journals and scientific observations. In the evening all joined in athletic and other games in a large hall. Hepburn became proficient in making soap and candles. The Canadians had a whim that it was a mysterious operation, and that its success was hindered if a woman approached the kettle. So Hepburn was rid of female intermeddlers at least, though the women got the best of it by being spared the heavy labor.

The new year, 1821, came in rather gloomily. The English tried to be merry, but the heart will be heavy on one scanty meal a day. In this state of things an ice-covered Canadian, sent ahead to herald Back's coming, cheered them with packages of letters from England and the news of approaching provisions. With spring the deer returned, and the hunt was rewarded with game.

They now made preparations for the journey to the Coppermine and the voyage on its waters to the sea. Their Indian chief promised to stock Fort Enterprise with provisions by the first of September for their use should they return that way.

On the 4th of June a party, under Dr. Richardson, started ahead, and Franklin followed soon after. The journey of nearly a month to the Coppermine was made one of great fatigue by heavy portages and scanty daily food. They all, however, safely embarked on the river.

For awhile their Indian chief and his followers accompanied them, making themselves useful by hunting excursions along the shore. Dr. Richardson keenly observed the shore as they passed for objects of scientific interest. He was surprised at the few fur-bearing animals in all their travels. The Indians had made so reckless a slaughter of them that they were nearly exterminated, so that but few beavers even were seen. He records in connection with this statement the following incident: One day an Englishman was out hunting this interesting creature. Soon he caught sight of five young beavers at play on a floating log. They were having an exciting frolic, in leaping upon the log, then pushing each other off, and scampering over their little play-ground. The sportsman crept softly up, sheltered by the bushes. As he raised his gun to fire, their innocent expression of face, and child-like affection and confidence, so reminded him of the children he had left at home, that he dropped at once his gun and a tear, and left them unharmed.

As the expedition approached the sea they came into the country of the Esquimo, the deadly enemies of the Indians. Franklin suggested to Akaitcho that it was a good time to make a treaty of peace. This he consented to do, but showed great fears the nearer he came to his enemies. On the other hand, the Esquimo fled the moment they saw the strangers. Finally, Akaitcho refused to go further, and returned to Fort Enterprise with his men, promising to meet Franklin's party there. The next day Mr. Wentzel and four Canadians were sent back to Slave Lake to forward dispatches to England, and to see that the

Indians were faithful to their engagement in reference to a supply of provisions.

Franklin was now in sight of the sea, and in the region of the musk-ox, several of which he killed. They had when attacked a singular, and for themselves, an unfortunate habit. They at once huddled together, as if feeling a sense of safety in being screened from their enemy by one another.

They arrived on the shore of the great Northern Oceans July 19, after a most painful and perilous journey of three hundred and thirty-four miles, one hundred and seventeen of which were made by dragging their canoes and stores overland.

They now paddled along the coast with their frail canoes. The shore for awhile afforded good landing-places, so that they could encamp at night. But soon a steep and high rocky point, against which broken ice was piled, turned them further out to sea. Just then a violent storm arose, the thunder crashed, and their canoes were frightfully tossed by the sea. They were compelled to seek the nearest hiding-place. They found a few seal, which were too shy for their hunters, and some small deer, which fell into their hands. But the deepest gloom rested upon the encampment. The season of the severest arctic cold was setting in, and birds and beasts were leaving the desolate shore, while the men, whose courage had been remarkable, began to grow faint-hearted. Franklin saw that an immediate return was a necessity. He had followed the shore-line nearly six hundred miles.

On their return voyage they went up a river they had passed a few days before, until they came to an impassable fall. Stopping here to make two small portable canoes of their two large ones, they started in as straight a line as possible for Fort Enterprise, one hundred and fifty miles distant. Their suffering from cold and hunger soon became too shocking to be detailed. An idea of it may be formed from the fact that they ate the leather and raw hide of their old shoes. Too weak to carry any burdens, Dr. Richardson's scientific specimens were thrown away, and, in spite of all remonstrance, the men abandoned the canoes. In these dreadful hours of want Franklin devoutly says: "We looked with humble confidence to the great Author and Giver of all good for the continuance of the support which had always been given to us at our greatest need."

When they came to the Coppermine they were detained nine days in constructing a raft on which to cross. Richardson, with a heroic devotion to the interest of his companions, proposed to swim the Coppermine, and carry a line tied around his body by which the raft could be drawn safely across. In attempting to carry into effect this proposal he nearly reached the opposite side, when, exhausted by swimming and chilled by cold, he sank. His companions drew him back by the rope in almost a lifeless state. They immediately rolled him in a blanket and placed him before a fire, when he revived sufficiently to give directions in further efforts for his recovery. It was many months before he entirely recovered.

When twenty-four miles from Fort Enterprise, Hood's strength entirely failed. Dr. Richardson and Hepburn agreed to stay by him, and try to nurse him for further effort, while Franklin pressed on with the rest of the party. Before parting all united in prayer, thanking God for the recent rescue from imminent danger of one of their number, and invoking Divine aid in further labor and peril.

When Franklin had gone on some distance, three Canadians, and Michel, an Indian, turned back. The Indian reached Richardson's camp, but the others, as he reported, had perished by the way of hunger and cold; but his conduct having been for some time strange, Hepburn expressed to Richardson the opinion that Michel had murdered the Canadians. While these painful thoughts were indulged, Michel shot Hood through the head when alone with him in the tent. Though the ball had plainly entered the *back* of its victim's head, Michel declared Hood had shot himself. The murderer was armed, and much stronger than the united strength of both white men, and used threatening language to them. In this awful state they lived for three days, the Indian watching every motion. But at last Richardson found an opportunity to save their own lives, and end the guilty career of the murderer by shooting him with a pistol.

Franklin, on reaching Fort Enterprise, found

8

neither food nor their promising friend, Akaitcho. Back had been there, and left a note saying he had gone after the chief, and, if need be, should push on to the next fort and hurry up supplies. After eighteen days of terrible suffering at the fort, in which many of the men died of starvation, Richardson and Hepburn dragged their emaciated forms into the presence of their companions. The reunited explorers shocked each other by their ghostly faces and sepulchral voices. Another week of starvation passed, in which two more Canadians died. The Englishmen, in all their weakness, never omitted their morning and evening religious service. Spending most of the day lying on the hard floor, for they had no beds, the one most able would read from God's Word comforting promises, and from "Bickersteth's Scripture Helps." There was a melancholy interest attached to the latter. It was given them by a pious lady before they left London, and was in poor Hood's hands when he was shot. How sweet the thought to his friends that some "Scripture Help" occupied his last earthly thoughts.

On the 7th of November three Indian messengers arrived from the ever-faithful and indomitable Back with supplies. These Indians not only brought food to the sufferers, but nursed them with untiring devotion, and conducted them slowly and cautiously to a place appointed by Back. Here were sledges and dogs and the comforts of the early days of their explorations, and by easy stages, stopping some months at Fort Chipeway, they reached York Factory in July, 1822, after an absence of three years, into which had been crowded many life-times of suffering, and during which they had traveled five thousand five hundred and fifty miles!

When they reached England honors and congratulations awaited them. Franklin had been made captain, Hood and Back lieutenants, and a post of honor, pay and comfort had been provided for Hepburn in the navy-yard.

CHAPTER XII.

A CHEERFUL ARCTIC WINTER.

IN May, 1821, while Franklin was in the midst of his overland expedition, of which we have just given an account, his friend Parry commenced his second voyage. It was hoped, as before, that they would find the north-west passage and meet.

We left Parry, on his return from Lancaster Sound, in the church with his officers and men, giving thanks to God for his guidance and preserving care. We shall see him putting his face again toward the icy regions, in the same devout spirit.

The flag-ship, this time, commanded by Parry, was the "Fury;" his second in command, Lieut. Lyon, took charge of the "Hecla." The ships fortunately possessed about the same capacity for sailing, which kept them together. Many of the officers and men of the first expedition were in this, and the utmost harmony prevailed.

An incident occurred, as the ships were sailing down the Thames, of a sad character, but bringing out the excellent Christian spirit of the commander. There was on board the "Fury" an old seaman by the name of John Gordon, a tall, well-proportioned man of great strength and activity. In the commencement of the former voyage he was like many sailors, rough, ready, profane, and coarse. But during the long ice-imprisonment at Melville Island, under the religious instruction of his commander, he was born of the Spirit. His Christian influence on shipboard promised now to be of the most positive character. But in attempting to throw a kedge-anchor from a boat the line attached to it became entangled round his body, jerked him overboard, and drowned him.

Parry, in writing to his parents soon after this, says: "I can safely say I never felt so strongly the vanity, uncertainty, and the comparative unimportance of every thing this world can give, and the paramount necessity of a preparation for another and a better life, than this."

No other incident worthy of note occurred to the discoverers until their arrival at the mouth of Hudson Strait. Here a supply transport, the "Nautilus," which came with them thus far, returned home with the last news.

Let the reader now turn to a good map of North America. He will see that Parry's *first* voyage was past this strait, through Davis Strait and Baffin Bay to Lancaster Sound, then due west to Melville Island. *Now* he proposed to go west, through Hudson Strait to Southampton Island, and then to work his way north through unexplored waters to the Polar Sea. It was a bold plan, and we shall see how bravely it was prosecuted.

The ships were soon enveloped in fogs. When these lifted they revealed a barren shore, dripping with melting ice, hills covered with snow, and whole fleets of icebergs, one counting fifty-four. A single berg, which attracted special attention, rose two hundred and fifty-eight feet above the sea. These crystal islands were no welcome sights to the strangers. When they ran a-tilt against each other, as they often did without warning, it would be neither pleasant nor safe to be between them. There was another performance which the bergs fancied, but the sailors did not; they occasionally launched into the sea a large part of one of their sides; this destroyed their balance, and they immediately turned something like a somersault. As the ships must of necessity sometimes go quite near the bergs, as there was never any advertisement when this performance would come off, and as it was attended by a great commotion in the sea, the whole thing was decidedly disagreeable.

They reached, through much toil, the south-east shore of Southampton Island; the next point at which they aimed was Repulse Bay, the most northern yet known water in this direction, lying a little west of the extreme north of this island. They pressed on up the nearest—the west—side, though the round-about way on the east side of the island was known to be much clearer of ice. Though sometimes decidedly warned off by the Ice King, they did enter Repulse Bay and found clear sailing. Sending up a shout for the north-west passage, they spread their sails for due west. But it proved a short trip to the land boundaries in that direction. A little crest-fallen, they came out of the bay and sailed north, observing every little inlet which turned west. At the entrance of one of these, which they named Lyon Inlet, after the second officer in command, they found a small island. As the season for further navigation was ended they cut a canal in the ice to the southern shore of this island, which they called Winter Island, and drew up their ships into winter-quarters.

They were better prepared with provisions, means of warming the vessels, and comforts every way, than on the first voyage. Once adjusted in their outward arrangements to their situation, Parry set in operation the means to interest and profit his men, and so to make them contented and happy. A thoughtful Christian lady had put on board a large and well-constructed magic lantern. This was set up, and afforded much amusement. The officers formed themselves into a musical band. Parry himself joined, as he claimed to be "a pretty tolerable" performer. After a little practice they treated the crews to free concerts. We presume their audience were delighted and not over critical.

But the Christian commander aimed not at amusement only. The lower decks of both ships were cleared, and made inviting school-rooms. Here, several evenings in each week, the men were taught reading and writing. At Christmas sixteen well-written copies were handed to the teachers by sailors who when the school began could not write a line. It was said by the commander, with great satisfaction, "Though many came out with me who did not know a letter, when we returned home there was not a man who could not read his Bible."

The position of the ships was in waters never before visited by white men, but Esquimo were soon found to be there. They at first viewed the strangers at a distance with agitation and wonder. When invited nearer they came on, running, skipping, and laughing, being well-nigh beside themselves with the strange things before them. But they were soon on easy terms with the sailors. The hand-organ and "fiddle" were put in operation, making them wild with delight. They sung and danced in their way, uproarious the while with laughter, in which the strangers joined heartily. At one time the fiddler was sent out upon the ice, and "all hands" joined in the dance, savages and white men, officers and sailors, making a sight "both rare and comic." The "figure" of the Esquimo consisted in stamping and jumping with all their strength. One young sailor, a fresh, ruddy fellow, excited the special attention of the Esquimo ladies. They patted him on the face, and danced about him in a ring. The natives were so excited generally that they became uproarious, cutting the most extraordinary capers, and acting as if they were drunk. One of their jokes was to come slyly up to the sailors, shout piercingly in one ear, and give the other a rousing slap, bursting at the same time into a loud laugh. The cook of the "Fury" was so fine a jumper that he was singled out for this kind of compliment. The poor fellow found his honors so uncomfortable that he had to flee to the ship to escape them. Parry says of himself: "While looking on I was sharply saluted in this manner, and, of course, was quite startled, to the great amusement of the bystanders."

One of the natives, glorying in his superior strength, and having thrown several of his countrymen in wrestling trials, tried his muscles on one of the officers. The officer was a strong man and skilled withal in the game, so that the Esquimo soon came in contact with the ice rather violently, at which the whole company set up a provoking laugh. But the vanquished champion, with admirable good sense, though rubbing his shins for pain, joined heartily in the merriment.

The same officer appointed himself teacher "of polite accomplishments." He took several Esquimo women and taught them to bow, courtesy, shake hands, turn their toes out, and put on drawing-room airs generally, master and pupils preserving the while the most becoming sobriety.

But the Esquimo had an eye to trade as well as fun. One day a company of their women came on board and sought the officers. As the thermometer was twenty degrees below zero, the white men were not surprised that their visitors were unusually well burdened with fur clothing; but their modesty was for a moment shocked when they began to undress in the open air. But they soon ascertained that the women had on several suits, the outer ones being intended for sale, they having put them on as a convenient way of getting their goods to market.

The Esquimo made loud protestations of honesty in their business visits, and we shall present some pleasing illustrations of a good claim being made to such professions. But exceptions would occur, and they were found to bear watching. One lady sold a single fur boot, but refused to sell the other though offered for it a good price. The zeal she showed in refusing naturally excited in the purchasers of fur boots "for ladies wear" a desire to obtain. But as the market was "tight" in this direction, the buyers rudely took the article by violence. It proved to be a valuable boot, containing two silver spoons and a pewter plate. The lady thief laughed heartily at the incident as a good joke, being sorry apparently only that she had not succeeded in getting off with her booty.

Soon after the visit of the Esquimo the explorers saw for the first time a village on the near shore, of snow huts. It burst upon them like stage scenery behind a suddenly drawn curtain. All wondered that not even the sharp look-out from the crow's nest had seen it before. But the Esquimo explained the mystery by putting one up in a few hours. They were constructed of smoothly cut blocks of snow, so adjusted as to make an architectural dome, the key-block going nicely into its place. It was entered by a hole at the side, into which a long tunnel was fitted. All who entered must get down upon their knees and creep through this tunnel, which was fastened up on the inside, when necessary, with a block of ice.

Inside there was a raised platform of snow around the sides. Upon this skins were thrown, making the sleeping-place for all the inmates. A hole was left in the top for ventilation, into which, when they wanted the cold shut out, they fitted a piece of clear ice. This answered for a window. A large bone was fixed across the ceiling, to which they hung a stone lamp. Seal oil and various kinds of fat were burned in this, affording a fire for all purposes. These simple people seem to build their homes by a kind of instinct, like the beaver, and when not in contact with a higher civilization, the same arrangement passes from father to son, essentially unchanged for generations.

Parry on a visit to one of the huts purchased the stone lamp of the housekeeper. She took it down, emptied out the oil, and wiped it out with a part of her dress. This not making it sufficiently clean to satisfy her tidy notion, she licked it out with her tongue.

Among the visitors to the ships was a woman of a very remarkable character. As her husband's name was Okotook, we will call her, in brief, Mrs. O., for her own name is hard to write or speak. Mrs. O. had a fine musical ear, and a soft, pleasant voice. She was expert with her needle, and neat and clean in all her work. She did not look at things new and wonderful to her with a vulgar stare, but was curious to know their use. Mrs. O. had another excellence still more wonderful for an Esquimo; she would not steal—at least, the strangers believed that she would not. Her honesty certainly shone in two or three incidents which are given in the narrative. Here is one. She had promised to cover for Parry a small model canoe, but as it was not done on time he charged her with a want of good faith. Her vehement gestures and face of injured innocence quite moved him. After a while an Esquimo came in with whom the canoe had been intrusted by Mrs. O. to bring it to the commander. She immediately charged him with the delinquency. Parry adds: "It is impossible for me to describe the quiet yet proud satisfaction displayed in her countenance in thus having cleared herself from a breach of promise."

Being well convinced of the superior intelligence of Mrs. O., it occurred to Parry that she might know something of the coast which he wished to explore. So he put paper and a pencil in her hand, and, with some difficulty, succeeded in making her understand what he desired. She began at once to fill sheet after sheet until she had filled a dozen with the outlines of the coast. The officers, who looked on with deep interest, saw her indicate the turn of the land to the west, giving a water communication in that direction. This chart was afterward proved to be essentially correct.

Mrs. O. had a son, Toolooak, who inherited his mother's gifts and strong natural affection. He would sit in the cabin of the "Fury" hours together, with pencil and paper, absorbed in sketching. His particular delight was in drawing animals, of which he seemed never tired.

Parry asked him one day if he would go to England with him.

"No!" he replied promptly, repeating it with emphasis many times. "No! If I should leave my father Okotook he would cry."

Okotook was at one time sick. His wife immediately manifested the deepest concern, sitting by him for hours with her hair disheveled, refusing food and rest. The physician of the expedition gave him a dose of medicine. It was his first dose, and he took it with great fear and agitation. Taking the cup in one hand he extended the other to his wife, who grasped it with both of hers. She evidently expected some great catastrophe to follow. But Okotook recovered, and great in their estimation was the white man's medicine.

Such is the remarkable picture given of Mrs. Okotook. But alas for the heathen! Before parting with her she developed to the strangers unmistakable traits of the savage. The reader will perceive more and more, as our narrative progresses, that the Esquimo, though having many amiable traits, and comparing favorably with any heathen on earth, are savages still, having but low moral sensibilities. How can it be otherwise since they see God so dimly.

We will give only a few additional touches to our picture of Esquimo life and character before leaving Winter Island for further discoveries.

Parry invited the belle of the tribe to sit for her

portrait, and when it was finished, he inquired of her and her husband what present he should make them for the favor. They both exclaimed, "A packet of tallow candles!" These being given, they immediately ate them! The wick of one, in going down, slightly embarrassed the lady, and Parry politely drew it out of her throat.

Commander Lyon invited an "intelligent" young Esquimo to dine with him. He was first instructed in the etiquette of the white man's table, and shown how to use a knife and fork and napkin. After dining, he was directed to the toilet stand to wash. He manifested such delight with the piece of perfumed Windsor soap that Lyon gave it to him. He laughed his thanks, and ate it on the spot.

We shall find in most of the Arctic voyages thrilling bear stories, some of them tragic, and others comic, but most of them having the matter-of-fact character of substantial meals to starving explorers. Here is a comic one. One of the Esquimo was busy in disengaging from his net a seal he had taken, when he felt a slap on his shoulder. Thinking it came from a companion, he continued to work. But a second slap caused him to look up, when, horrors! a grim old bear sat on his haunches with uplifted paws and open mouth directly over him; he seemed to say, "My good fellow, don't trouble yourself further about this seal; I'll take it off your hands!" The immediate result was a healthy run by the Esquimo, and a good meal on seal's flesh by the bear. We cannot say that we think the transaction was exactly fair on the bear's part, but these things took place in a heathen land.

The merry winter at Winter Island was not succeeded by an early spring nor a successful summer. Sickness came just before navigation could be resumed, and three men died. In July the expedition sailed up Fox Channel, and, after many failures, much delay, and several land excursions, the ships got into a narrow lead of water, at first free from ice. It soon, however, presented a field of "soft ice," through which, for some time, they forced the ship by crowding on all sail. Parry had seen from a high point on shore to which he had climbed an open sea beyond this strait, and this, of course, inspired intense desire to push through. But, alas! they soon ran against solid ice, where they remained for another winter. They named the place Igloolik. A second Arctic winter may be endured, but it seems impossible for it to be enjoyed. The third summer's toil did not yield great results, but Parry was sure the water he was in was either the Polar sea or an arm of it, though we may see by the map that he was not as near it by several degrees as when on his first voyage. So strong was his conviction that he had almost grasped success, that he proposed confidentially to Commander Lyon to spend a third winter in the Arctic ice. His plan was to send Lyon home in the "Hecla" with dispatches, and remain himself in the "Fury," and push north the following summer. He even prepared his dispatches, saying to the home authorities that he should undoubtedly come home by way of Kamchatka. This was plucky, but human energy is nothing when opposed to the defiance of ice and cold. These sent the scurvy among the men of the "Fury" and "Hecla," and they turned their prows homeward, which they were glad to reach in October, 1823, having been gone three summers and two winters.

CHAPTER XIV.

ARCTIC REVIVAL WORK.

WE have found Captain Parry a pleasant and profitable guide in our excursions into the regions of cold, and as we are assured we shall not find his enthusiasm nor excellence of character diminished, we will follow him to the end of his career as an explorer.

He remained at home only about six months after the close of his second voyage, and during a part of this time he was prostrate with sickness. In May, 1824, he sailed again with the "Fury" and "Hecla," this time choosing the "Hecla" as his flag-ship, the "Fury" being commanded by Lieutenant Hoppner. Prince Regent Inlet was to be the waters through which the north-west passage was now to be sought. The reader will see it just north of Boothia Bay, near which he spent the last winter of his late voyage. To reach it, however, he proposed to take his first route through Lancaster Sound.

As the details of this are much like those of the other expeditions, we shall only dwell upon a few striking incidents.

It was Sunday morning in Davis Strait. All were assembled for Divine service except those required to sail the ship; now, as she often had done, bravely fighting the ice. Parry had nearly ended a sermon he was reading, when the quarter-master crept up to him with evident agitation, and whispered a few hurried words. The commander, without betraying any emotion, asked a few questions in a low tone, and sent him back to his post of duty, continuing his reading, as though nothing had happened. The sermon finished, the Divine blessing implored, he raised his hand and said :—

"Now, my lads, all hands on deck—but mind, no bustle!"

The fog had cleared up during the service, and the ship was heading toward the land. The captain, judging from what the quarter-master reported that there was time to finish the service, now took his place of command, and the ship was soon out of danger.

"I knew we could trust our captain!" exclaimed one of the sailors, wiping a tear from his weather-beaten face.

The vessels reached Regent Inlet in September, and attempted to sail south. This was precisely what they attempted to do in the same place on the first voyage in 1819, but were prevented doing by the ice; they found now the same unyielding barrier, and were forced into winter-quarters on the east side of the inlet, near its mouth. Here were no Esquimo and no animals, but plenty of cold, ice, and utter desolation. Besides, most of the men had experienced three Arctic winters, so that the "fun of the thing" was gone, but the awful silence of the long night, and the oppressive dreariness, remained. But how strange are God's ways! and good as strange! This dark winter was the occasion, to many of the men, of the coming into their hearts of the light which shineth more and more unto the perfect day! Even to Captain Parry it commenced a new era of Christian experience. The fact may be thus briefly stated:—

On his return from his last voyage he learned that, during his absence, his father had died. This deeply affected him, as his home ties had been of a remarkably strong character, and his affection for his father very intense. It created in him searching self-examination, and new aspiration in the Divine life.

Fortunately for the further cultivation of this frame of mind, the purser of the "Hecla," a Mr. Hooper, was a man of deep experience in the spiritual life, and of unceasing Christian activity. Between the captain, therefore, and his purser there sprung up a close Christian friendship, and many Arctic hours passed swiftly by while they were conversing of the higher Christian life.

Parry commenced now a careful, thorough study of the New Testament, applying its truths to his own heart as he had never done. Thus seeking, he found the blessing of a greater measure of the Spirit. He says of the result: "'The entrance of the word giveth light;' so it was in my experience." He speaks especially of his increased apprehension of Christ as received into the heart by faith, and as the only means of entrance into the "narrow way."

Thus blessed in a Christian helper, and thus enlarged in his own experience, his labors for the spiritual welfare of his men could but be attended with marked results.

The schools, now having the zealous labors of Mr. Hooper, became at once so popular that all the men of both ships attended them. Parry says: "They made such a scene of quiet occupation as I never before witnessed on board a ship."

Mr. Hooper's journal affords us the following glance at one of the Sunday evening meetings: "I have been this evening gratified beyond measure by the conduct of my school. We assembled as usual, and Captain Parry read to us an excellent sermon. We then read over three or four times the second lesson of the day, and I expounded it to the best of my ability. After this we went to prayers, and having closed, I wished them good-night as usual, when my friend John Darke, a seaman of the 'Hecla,' said he wished to say a few words. He then dropped upon his knees, and in a few simple but affecting words returned thanks for the blessings enjoyed by himself and shipmates in a Christian captain and a Christian teacher, imploring the blessing of God upon Captain Parry and myself. After this he desired for himself and his shipmates to thank me for the trouble I had taken. The countenances of every one spoke the same thing, and showed that Darke had been put forward by them to utter these kind words."

This Darke, some time after the return of the ship, acknowledged, in a letter to Hooper, that the instruction he received in the "Hecla" was the means "of saving his soul."

Thus passed the winter. The spring was occupied in part by exploring parties in various directions. It was not until July that the ships were afloat and the voyage renewed. But it was soon brought to a disastrous close. The "floes," great masses of ice, were in active operation, forced on by stormy currents and high winds. One of these seized both ships and tossed them upon the shore as if they had been its playthings. They were got off at high water, but the "Fury" was in a sinking condition. All hands worked at the pumps until they were exhausted in body and bewildered in mind. The "Hecla" came to her rescue, but she continued in a desperate condition until finally she went ashore again a hopeless wreck.

All hands were now piled into the "Hecla," leaving no room for additional stores from the "Fury." Thus situated there was no course left to the disappointed Parry but to return home. The season was yet early, the sea open southward, and it seemed to him like turning his back upon the long-sought prize.

Though unsuccessful in the main object of his voyages, Parry had added, more than any other explorer, to the geographical knowledge of the polar regions. This was appreciated, and, even now, fresh honors were showered upon him. But he turned from these to let his new Christian light shine in active, self-denying labor for the salvation of souls. From henceforth many were to know him as a faithful Christian, who would never have known him as the brave, successful navigator. This change, he says, made him the subject of many sneers; but he could well afford to receive these unmoved, having the approbation of the good and the smile of his Master.

While thus working for Christ, Parry married a daughter of Sir John Stanley, who seems to have entered into all his labors.

But his enthusiasm for polar exploration was unabated. A sledge journey from Spitzbergen to the northern ice center was now all the talk. The suggestion is said to have come from Scoresby, the intelligent and brave captain of a whaler, whom we have met before. Parry and Franklin had conversed together concerning the proposal. So, early in the spring of 1827, Parry was sent in his well-tried "Hecla," with a picked crew, to make the bold experiment.

Their departure from England was honored by a "flag raising" on board, by his wife, and by the presence and blessing of many friends. The ship touched at a port in Norway and took in eight reindeer and a supply of their moss provender. With these they expected to make long and rapid journeys over level if not smooth ice; to this end they received lessons in their management and care from the Norwegians.

Having reached a point a little north of Spitzbergen, they committed the "Hecla" to her ice-prison and hoisted out their two boats, the "Endeavor" and "Enterprise." These were each twenty feet long by seven wide; they were finished with a floor inside affording a good sleeping-place; runners were so framed that the boats could be placed upright upon them; a water-proof canvas covering was provided; wheels and fixtures to make a carriage of them were stowed away among the freight; and the material and workmanship of all were of the best character.

They were thus prepared to sail, slide along on runners, or trundle ahead on wheels.

Disappointment and baffled plans are always in order in the icy regions. Instead of something like a plain, and a solid continent of ice, as other explorers had seen, or thought they saw, our voyagers were confronted at the start by ugly hummocks—jagged piles of ice—and drifting floes. The reindeer could be of no use and they were left behind, probably as junks of frozen venison for future use. Having spent some weeks in short explorations, and in deferred hope of a better condition of traveling, the boat excursionists left the ship in the middle of June. There was at the moment an open, smooth sea, and they sailed away joyfully through eighty miles. Then came floes, small and separated by open spaces of water, so that now they traveled by alternately dragging the boats along the ice, and launching them for a sail.

Parry adopted a novel method of dividing the working time; they slept by day and journeyed by night. By this arrangement they avoided the glare, which caused a troublesome snow blindness, and had the warmest part of the twenty-four hours for sleeping. It worked well.

They arose in the early evening, attended to family prayers; breakfasted on warm cocoa and biscuit, cooked by a fire of spirits of wine, their only fuel; changed their dry sleeping furs and boots for the wet ones of the night before, and they were ready for a start. They made it a point to have dry clothes to sleep in, but did not mind drawing on a wet or frozen boot in the morning, for if it was dry, it was sure to be wet soon after starting. They stopped at midnight to dine, at daybreak they supped, chatted, said their prayers, and went to sleep to be awoke by the sound of a bugle in the evening. They tried hard to make the night pleasant and successful, and the day a time of sleep.

But the explorers spent their strength for naught and labored in vain, for while *they* were toiling over the extended ice-rafts toward the north, these rafts were drifting south. Once, after five days of seeming good progress, the officers took an observation and ascertained that they had advanced eight miles. Worse than this, they sometimes tramped miles northward to find themselves farther south than when they started. This was a rough joke of the grim Ice King, who seemed to put his finger to his nose and say with a ghastly smile: "Beautiful progress! you must persevere to the pole!" But they did not, for having reached *almost* to the eighty-third degree of north latitude

—farther in that direction than civilized man had ever before gone—they turned round. On the back trip they shot and ate bears, the rightful owners of the *soil.* But these natives were equally unscrupulous; for the strangers, when they arrived at Table Island, where they had deposited supplies, ascertained that the white polars had eaten all they wanted, which was just the amount they found.

The expedition arrived home safely in September, and thus ended Sir Edward Parry's arctic experience.

CHAPTER XV.

LOST AND FOUND.

WHILE Parry was making his third voyage in the north-west, and his sledge journey in the north-east, Franklin was on a second land expedition. He and his friend Richardson took the great Mackenzie River this time, and sailed down to its entrance into the Polar Sea. Here they separated, Franklin going west, hoping to reach Bering Strait, or, at least, Icy Cape, near the dividing line of the British and the Russian—now the United States—possessions; Richardson going east to survey the coast to the Coppermine. Lieutenant Beechey, in the mean time, was sent in a ship to Bering Strait, to work his way east to Icy Cape and meet Franklin. The voyager from the Mackenzie did not quite reach Icy Cape, but Beechey's boats passed it and were within one hundred and sixty miles of Franklin when insurmountable barriers turned him back. The expeditions had essentially the same incidents as that we have narrated, only, having the advantage of their former experience, and having at the start a better outfit, their sufferings were far less.

About ten years had passed away, filled with many stirring events relating to the arctic regions, since Captain John Ross's unfortunate return from

Lancaster Sound. His then subordinate officer, Parry, had earned in the time, and retired upon, his laurels. Ross, a really brave commander, chafed under the public censure imposed upon him. In fact, it seemed harsh, and he had many sympathizing friends. They desired for him, as he desired for himself, an opportunity to retrieve his reputation. But the Government was out of breath with its hot haste to get to the north pole. Besides, whether their enterprises succeeded or failed, they cost great sums in gold and silver, and many lives. So, having tried Parry and Franklin, in whom the nation had unqualified confidence, and who had done much, they would not try one who had failed where he might have succeeded. So Ross turned from the Government to a friend; that friend, in his mental distress, was Felix Booth, a wealthy merchant. He had been desirous for some years to send Ross to the arctic regions on the resources of his ample purse, but he would not do it because the Government had offered a hundred thousand dollars to any one who should discover the north-west passage. He would not be looked upon as seeking the golden bribe rather than honor and the public good. But when, in 1828, the Government withdrew the offer, he set about the preparations of an exploration. He laid down for the expense eighty-five thousand dollars; Ross himself added fifteen thousand more, and the material aid was supposed to be secured. But what expensive amusements these arctic journeys are! This goodly sum, as we shall see, purchased the means of only a small expedition.

The "Victory," a Liverpool merchant-ship, was bought, and sent into the dock to have her hull toned up with the best of oak and iron for the arctic fight. She was also adjusted to a steam-engine. The steam-engine was an infant at this time; it was, therefore, expecting too much of it to suppose it could withstand such terrible foes as those found at the extreme north.

On the 23d of May, 1829, the "Victory" steamed down the Thames; but her engine broke down, and she paused at the Isle of Man for repairs. She was again delayed by an accident to her engineer. A supply-vessel, the "John," had been employed to go with them to the mouth, or thereabouts, of Prince Regent Inlet, and having deposited for them her cargo of stores, to scud home before the ice fetters were thrown around it. But these delays caused her crew to see an arctic winter as one of the contingencies quite too likely to happen, and they flatly refused to go. So Ross sailed with only the "Victory" and a small cargo of supplies, less than he expected.

Science of our day, with its ocean-steamers of wonderful capacity, may, perhaps, laugh at the "Victory's" steam-engine. When fairly at sea it kept the captain and other officers up to aid the engineer to keep its rickety joints together. The sailors had to turn out at night to blow the bellows to keep up steam, and to gather ice for the boiler. We hope Jack didn't swear profanely at this new mode of sailing! We know he did a better thing; at the welcome orders from the quarter-deck he pitched the troublesome thing into the sea!

Having reached South Greenland, the "Victory" ran into a Danish port for the purchase of a further outfit for arctic winters. They were soon on friendly terms with the governor, the religious teacher, and the Christianized Esquimo. There was lying in the harbor the hull of a London vessel recently wrecked. Ross purchased her stores, and was thus fully provisioned; this additional supply probably saved the explorers from ultimate starvation.

They found Lancaster Sound and Barrow Strait nearly free from ice, and reached the beach in Prince Regent Inlet, on which the wreck of the "Fury" was left by Parry; but nothing of it could be found. The tent-poles remained, and near them the casks, tightly sealed, of sugar, meat, flour, cocoa, and other provisions, left by Parry nearly four years before. All were in good order, although the bears had left evidence that they had tried upon the casks the strength of their teeth and paws. Here was another timely addition to their supplies; there were twenty-three men to be fed, and had they then known the length of time they were to depend upon these provisions, they would have been even more thankful that bruin's teeth and claws had not opened the casks.

They found the navigation favorable, so they did not stop long at Fury Beach, but cruised south on the western side of the inlet, passing through a strait into a large gulf which Ross named after his patron, Boothia. Sailing on they reached its southern extremity, nearly opposite the Fury and Hecla Strait, where Parry had spent a winter during his second expedition. Here they found a good harbor, and seeing signs of the rapid approach of the winter prohibition of all activity of either ship or men, they prepared to spend the season's imprisonment in it. They first cut for their vessel a canal, so as to bring her near the shore, involving a long and tedious work. The powder and many of the stores were then removed to a sheltered place on the land. To make their home in the ship warm and dry they resorted to several very ingenious Yankee-like contrivances. Covering their deck, first with snow two and a half feet thick, and stamping it down until it became as solid as ice, they then spread over it a dry sand from the shore, making something like a gravel-walk. They then banked up with snow the ship's sides, and roofed the deck over with canvas.

The vapor of the cabins, instead of being allowed to condense, and thus keep every thing damp and cold, except at the expense of a great amount of fuel and a high temperature, was conducted through the upper deck into the open air by tubes. Over the mouth of these tubes iron-tanks were placed, the open side down. The tanks being in an atmosphere averaging many degrees below zero, the vapor as it reached them froze solid. This they cut out and carried below, thus not only keeping their apartments dry, but securing a supply of fresh-water ice. The air necessary to make the fires burn was brought in copper tubes directly to the fire-place, and so warmed before it was distributed through the cabin. Two anterooms were made, the outer one for the men's wet clothes.

Their supply of provisions, on examination, was ascertained to be sufficient for two years, used liberally, and could be made to last three years. The health and spirits of the men were, therefore, kept up by three meals a day, and plenty to do.

With these happy sufficiencies there was one fortunate lack; only a small quantity of liquor remained. Ross, like a sensible man, though in this respect ahead of his age, declared on the spot that he believed that without it his men would endure the cold better, and be less likely to be attacked by their terrible enemy, the scurvy. Under the counsel of so good an adviser, the men cheerfully and at once agreed to dispense entirely with their "grog," and reserve it for strictly medicinal purposes.

Divine service was daily performed, the Sabbath regarded by the omission of unnecessary work, divine service for all, and a special service in the evening—a kind of Sunday-school—for the sailors. Every week-day evening the secular schools were in operation.

Thus far Ross' expedition was a success. He had surveyed three hundred miles of hitherto undiscovered coast, and reached a point within two hundred and eighty miles of Franklin's furthest eastern journey from the mouth of the Coppermine.

As they had sailed along the coast they had observed traces of Esquimo, but seen none. Whales had fearlessly played about the ship, not yet taught to be shy by the deadly harpoon.

Having become fairly settled, the men turned their attention to hunting. Bears and wolves were not plenty, but caused occasionally a healthy excitement. Foxes were more abundant, and were sometimes trapped, though the arctic fox has the cuteness of his relative of warmer climates in keeping out of harm's way. The seal-traps were more successful; the seal oil and skins proved very useful, and so would their flesh, if the explorers had experienced the extreme hunger of many later visitors to those regions.

Sea-fowl were quite plenty; one species of gull, the kittiwake, attracted special attention by its rare beauty. Its bill was lemon-color, its plumage a blending of ash, black, and white, and its legs livid.

Commander James Ross, a nephew of the captain, who had accompanied his uncle, proved an expert hunter, and, in fact, every way an efficient officer.

In January a report of the "Victory's" cannon brought to the explorers a welcome company of Esquimo. They were shy at first, but on the approach of Captain Ross, they formed in a kind of military order, brandishing their spears and knives. The captain shouted some friendly words in their own language, which he had learned elsewhere, and they immediately sent back the kind salutation. Ross threw away his gun and repeated "Aja tima!" The Esquimo shouted "Aja tima," tossed aside their spears and knives, and were soon on excellent terms with the white faces.

There were women and children among the visitors. The mothers generally carried their babies in a big fur hood which hung from the back of their neck; but sometimes they adopted a mode of carrying these household treasures which is not usual, we think, even with the Esquimo—they tucked them away in their boots!

One of their young men was drawn on a sledge, he having but one leg; the other had been amputated in the following *savage* way: The upper part of the leg was first bound tightly with strips of hide; the flesh of the lower part was then cut off with their dull, clumsy knives, and the bone was slipped into a hole in the ice and snapped off! We hope the doctor did not charge heavily for this kind of surgery! The surgeon of the "Victory" kindly made the young man a wooden leg, on which he strutted about, with the most extravagant expressions of delight.

When April 1830 came, the discoverers were astir; some made a special business of hunting, game being now more abundant, and the necessity for fresh provisions more urgent; others were off on exploring excursions, in two parties—one led by Captain Ross, and the other by Commander James Ross. The commander was the man of greater enterprise, and general knowledge; he was wide awake in securing scientific as well as geographical knowledge. His excursions were especially directed to finding a passage out of the gulf where they were, in a westerly direction. But the most intelligent natives assured them that the only way into the sea beyond was farther north, meaning through Barrow Strait, already discovered by Parry.

All of the excursions of the younger Ross were made with dog-sledges, and Esquimo as guides. After having been out with them several times, he and the surgeon visited their camp to get guides for further exploration. Instead of the usual friendly greeting, the men met them, armed with knives and spears, and with angry faces. One old man was especially excited, and rushed at the visitors with his spear, but was restrained by his son. The women and children huddled together, aside, evidently expecting a scene, and the men formed a line abreast, grasping their spears and knives. Ross could get no explanation of this show of a bloody fight, and affairs with the strangers were becoming critical. They had each a loaded gun, but they were reluctant to shoot down men who had been, up to this time, fast and valuable friends, and were even now evidently acting under some serious misunderstanding. But to prevent being stabbed and overpowered, the officers brought their guns to their shoulders and their fingers to the locks. One look at the muzzle of the guns was happily quite enough for the timid foe. They, probably, had seen the lightning blazing from them, heard their thunder, and seen them deal death to the wild beasts. They broke and ran like sheep. The women then approached with friendly signs, and Ross succeeded in getting this explanation of the threatening incident: The old man, whose resentment was so intense, had just lost a son by the falling of a stone on his head. Their medicine man had attributed the fatal accident to the witchcraft of the white faces; therefore their braves were bent on revenge.

Ross succeeded in restoring confidence, the frightened men came back, guides were readily obtained, and the explorers went on their way.

The excursion, however, proved a sad one. Their provisions failed, and they were obliged to kill and eat seven of their nine dogs. This resort is much like taking the wheels from a carriage for fuel when on a long journey. The men were longer in getting back, having to draw the sledges instead of riding, and when at last they reached the ship they were but skeleton men.

Thus the summer wore away, and the "Victory" was still bound with ice fetters. August came, promised them freedom and an open sea, broke its promise and departed. September stepped forward with *melting* sunbeams, loosened the bands of the imprisoned ship, and she sailed joyously from Felix Harbor, where she had spent eleven months; but the breezes had only well filled the sails, and her prow felt its renewed power to cut through the waves, when she struck a rock! In breathless suspense all awaited the result, when she swung off and started again, but only to ground in the sand, where she seemed inclined to stay. Quickly as possible she was lightened by removing the stores to the shore. With deep anxiety they watched the effect of the returning tide; and when it was shouted, "She floats! she floats!" every heart bounded for joy.

With all sails spread, they sailed away—four miles, and, night coming on, Captain Ross fastened his ship to an iceberg, as if he had not been icebound enough, and waited for the morning. The morning came, but not the sailing; they were once more held firmly in the grip of the Ice King. Many laborious days were spent in sawing the thick, firm ice, and warping the ship through the canal thus made; when reaching a comparatively sheltered place near their old quarters, they spent another winter.

The only noticeable incident of this winter was the discovery by the scientific, younger Ross, of the long-sought "Western Magnetic Pole"—a spot where the needle of the compass dipped and stood still. The discoverer was in ecstasies, and thus records his feelings: "I leave my readers to imagine my transports; all my perils and fatigues were forgotten, and I felt as if I had nothing to do but to go home and be happy for the rest of my days."

The explorers built as good a monument to mark the spot as the circumstances allowed, putting a sealed canister beneath it containing documents relating to the discovery. Their *feelings* prompted them to build a monument over it as high as an Egyptian pyramid. But, after all, later science has shown that this discovery was of no practical value.

The second winter passed and the third summer came, bringing great labor, much suffering from cold, and insufficient food, and constant "hope deferred." When in August they were under sail again, they made, as during the preceding year, a few miles only, and then were again frozen tight for a third winter. Three weeks of navigation in a year, and a progress of four miles, they wisely concluded would not pay, so they decided to take to the boats and sledges and make their escape the quickest and easiest way possible as soon as the third winter should be ended. Therefore when April, 1832, arrived, they began to move out of the "Victory" toward Fury Beach, a distance of one hundred and eighty miles in a direct line, and three hundred by the windings. The goods they needed to carry being many and heavy, and their strength small, they took light loads, carried them a short distance and then set them down to return for more, thus going over the same ground two or three times a day. The first month they made thirty miles in a direct line, but had traveled, including the repeated journeys and the windings to avoid hummocks, three hundred and twenty-nine miles. During this month terrific storms of wind had hurled the sleet into their faces and piled the snow in their path.

They now made their last journey to the ship,

nailed her colors to the mast, and bade her farewell.

When they reached a point near enough to Fury Beach, where, it will be recollected, Parry's ship "Fury" had been wrecked, and where there was now a deposit of boats and provisions, the main party halted, built a temporary shelter, and rested. Commander Ross soon pressed on, with a few picked men, to Fury Beach, to examine the condition of things and to return. The captain moved forward with the main body more slowly; young Ross meeting them on his return with the good report that the store of provisions were in good order, and, though some of the boats had been washed away, enough remained for their purpose. On the first of July the whole party reached Fury Beach. Having now access to a larger stock of provisions, they ate hearty meals, rested, and recruited. They called their canvas-mansion Somerset House.

Having spent a month at this place, getting ready to man the boats for further progress to Baffin Bay through Barrow Strait, they bid adieu, as they hoped, to the Somerset House. But they only got well into Barrow Strait when they were driven back to the Somerset House to spend yet another winter. This fourth winter, amid arctic darkness, cold, and short provisions, was the most fearful of all; but yet only one man died.

All felt, when the next traveling season arrived, that they must reach the waters of the whalers and be rescued by them, or perish. With this feeling they had, by incredible labor and endurance, got out of Regent Inlet once more, passed Cape York, wound along the water lanes in the ice until they had reached Navy Board Inlet, which we may find on the map, about half way between Cape York and Baffin Bay. They drew their boats to land, pitched a tent, ate their supper, went through with the Divine service, in which, we doubt not, they introduced the prayer: "Lord, preserve our lives, and bring us again to our homes and friends." At four in the morning the watch startled all by the thrilling shout, "A sail! a sail!"

The boats were manned, and with all of their little strength, now stimulated to almost desperate exertions, they rowed out to sea, making every possible signal to attract attention. But the ship kept on her course, not seeing them, and was soon out of sight. A sullen despair, which precedes the fatal crisis, was settling down upon the crew, when Captain Ross shouted, what he scarcely dared believe, "Another sail!" After a little pause, and almost breathless suspense, he added: "Yes, she bears down upon us; we are seen!" and "we are saved!" was soon added as the sail drew nearer. The wind subsiding, the ship lowered her boat, commanded by her mate. As he approached Ross he said inquiringly:—

"You have lost your ship, sir?"

"Yes, we beg you would take us in. What is the name of your vessel?"

"The 'Isabella,' once commanded by Captain Ross."

"I am that Captain Ross, and these men are the crew of the 'Victory.'"

"Impossible!" was the quick reply. "Captain Ross has been dead these two years!"

But Ross was satisfied that he had the best information on this point, and it was not difficult to satisfy the mate and his captain of the fact.

When the facts were known on board the "Isabella" she received her old commander with a tumult of joy. When all were on board there followed a scene, says Captain Ross, so ludicrous that it drove for the moment all serious thoughts away. All were in a frame of mind to be amused: "Every man was hungry and was to be fed; all were ragged and were to be clothed; there was not one to whom washing was not indispensable, nor one whose beard did not deprive him of all human semblance. All was to be done at once: it was shaving, washing, dressing, eating, all intermingled; it was all the materials of each jumbled together, while in the midst of all there were interminable questions to be asked and answered on both sides—the adventures of the 'Victory,' our own escapes, the politics of England, and the news, now to us four years old."

But night came, and all was comparatively quiet. The sick had been cared for, the hungry fed, the ragged clothed, the unwashed cleansed, and, of course, all—and they were many—of the desponding among the explorers comforted. The rescued tried to sleep, but the beds were too warm and comfortable. Ross says of himself that he had to

Ross' Rescue.

leave his berth for a harder place before he could sleep.

The explorers arrived in London on the 19th of October, 1833, having been absent four years. Honors and emoluments were plentifully bestowed upon them. The officers were promoted, Captain Ross receiving a "knighthood," and his nephew a captaincy; the sailors received double pay, and the Parliament, the next year, returned to Ross his fifteen thousand dollars, with an addition of ten thousand—the goodly sum of twenty-five thousand. His patron, Felix Booth, they made *Sir* Felix.

The shout of the nation seemed to be, The lost is found! and they killed the fatted calf.

CHAPTER XVI.

DOWN THE GREAT FISH RIVER.

THE long absence of Capt. Ross excited great alarm in England. Though his expedition was one of private enterprise, and he had not been a favorite of the masses as an explorer, yet now that he was believed to be a suffering prisoner in the arctic ice, or already, with his men, a victim of cold and starvation, great and universal sympathy was felt. Men in high places of authority and influence began to talk, in 1832, of sending an expedition in search of him. The government finally determined to do it. When Back, who was in Italy at the time, heard of this decision, he hastened home and was accepted as its commander. He will be recollected by the reader as a hero in the two land expeditions of Franklin. He was now expected to go over a part of the routes of those journeys, reach the Polar Sea through the Great Slave Lake and the Great Fish River, then work his way east toward Prince Regent Inlet, over unknown land and waters, in hope to meet Ross or learn his fate. Such a journey was easily marked out on paper, and was very nice to talk about in the comfortable parlors of the great men. It was just the enterprise, too, to inspire the enthusiasm of the daring, skillful, and persistent Back.

He left England February, 1833, with Dr. King, who went as surgeon and naturalist. They were honored and cheered forward as they passed through New York city, and sailed up the Hudson to Albany. At Montreal they added to their company Canadians, four volunteers from the artillery service, and an old Indian boat-manager and guide by the name of Paul.

In two canoes, Paul guiding the leading one, they shot down the St. Lawrence to the Ottawa, and then ascended that river in a north-westerly direction. There were many water-falls and rapids for them to pass, some enchantingly beautiful, others impressively grand, but all imposing exhausting labor upon the explorers. The canoes and their freight had to be carried overland round these descending waters, the goods often in little parcels, and so in frequent return trips, and the canoes lifted up precipitous rocks and through tangled forests.

These water-falls are about as troublesome to the voyagers in descending the rivers as in ascending, and much more dangerous. Back tells the following story of the experience of some Indian acquaintance which illustrates this danger: A party were approaching a landing-place from which they were to carry the canoe round a grand cataract. In order to reach the landing they were obliged to go round a point of land which extended into the rapids, a short distance only from the edge of the falls. A strong oarsman stood in the bow; another, erect also and watchful, stood in the stern. They reached the point, fearlessly struck out into the rushing current, and with a few vigorous strokes, which threw the spray high over their heads, came round under the lee of the land. The sheltered landing was nearly reached, the danger seemed past, and the oarsmen relaxed their vigilance. Suddenly an eddy swung the prow of the canoe round and it darted out into the current. Swift as an arrow, it shot toward the cataract until it seemed to hang over its very edge. But the Indians, experienced in this kind of peril, were masters of the situation. They struck their paddles deep into the water, and with the desperate strength of men working for life they brought the canoe to a stand, and inch by inch moved off until the quiet waters of the landing were reached. They then landed on shore, drew up their canoe, threw themselves on the grass to rest, grunted their satisfaction, and cherished the recollection of the incident to relate around their camp-fires.

But the perils of the rivers were not the only ones our explorers encountered. Their comfort was often destroyed and their lives put in jeopardy by myriads of sand-flies. They covered every exposed part of their persons with blood-thirsty rapacity. To brush them off was only to remove those which were already gorged, or in part filled, for those with keener appetites. For every one killed, thousands came to avenge his death. It was a conflict waged by the explorers in which they were sure to be beaten. The Indians threw themselves on the ground, and fairly roared with anguish. Back adds ;—

"As we marched into the confined and suffocating chasms, or waded through the close swamps, they rose in clouds, actually darkening the air. To see or to speak was equally difficult, for they rushed at every undefended part, and fixed their poisonous fangs in an instant. Our faces streamed with blood, as if leeches had been applied, and there was a burning and irritating pain, followed by immediate inflammation, producing giddiness, which almost drove us mad, and caused us to moan with pain and agony."

Some of the Indians seemed to regard these tormentors with superstitious reverence. When Back at one time endeavored to smoke them out, an old Indian shook his head. "Bad," he muttered, "very bad! The great white chief"—referring to Franklin—"did not do so. He never killed a fly."

"This," says Back, "was true of Franklin. He quietly blew the gorged insects from his hands, saying, 'The world is wide enough for both of us.'"

The first most important stopping-place was Fort Chipeway, on the Athabasca Lake, where the reader has been several times with Franklin and others. This is distant from Montreal at least two thousand miles, the way they had traveled. It was now the middle of July, and they desired to push on, if possible, as far as the Great Fish River, flowing, as they believed, out of the Great Slave Lake into the sea. Their number had been increased, just before arriving at Fort

Chipeway, by a Mr. M'Leod, an old *employé* of the Hudson Bay Company, who brought along his wife and three children. A fine romantic journey for women and boys and girls did this exploring expedition afford! It was after their manner of life, so we do not hear that they either loitered behind or fainted by the way.

Before starting from this point let us look at the company Back had gathered about him, and at their "fixings." He says: "At my feet was a rolled bundle in oil cloth containing three blankets, called a bed; near it a piece of dried buffalo, fancifully ornamented with long black hairs, which, alas! no art can prevent from insinuating themselves between the teeth as you laboriously masticate the tough, hard flesh; then a tolerably clean napkin, spread, by way of a table-cloth, on a red piece of canvas, and supporting a tea-pot, some biscuits, and a salt-cellar; near this a tin plate; close by a square kind of a box or safe of the same material, rich with a pale, greasy hair, the produce of the colony at Red River; and the last, the far renowned *pemmican*, the best food of the country for expeditions such as ours. Behind me were two boxes containing astronomical instruments, and a sextant lying on the ground by a washing apparatus, a gun, an Indian shot-pouch, bags, basins, and an unhappy-looking japanned pot, whose sad bumps seemed to reproach me for many a bruise endured upon the rocks and portages.

"My crew were not less motley than the tent.

It consisted of Englishmen, Canadians, two metifs or half-breeds, and three Iroquois Indians. Babel could not produce a worse confusion of inharmonious sounds."

Having arrived at Fort Resolution, just south of the Great Slave Lake, Back took four of his crew to press on to the Great Fish River, while M'Leod came on with the rest, to some point on the north-east side of the lake, where he was to prepare winter-quarters.

Back was successful in finding the outlet of the river from the lake, and sailed a few days on its waters. This Great Fish River now bears Back's own name. He was delighted with his success thus far. He seemed to see a triumphant voyage on its waters to the sea when, in the spring, he should renew his explorations. With these feelings he turned back to Fort Reliance, as he called the spot where M'Leod had prepared winter-quarters.

Here he found not only his own company, but a starving troop of Indians who had come to hang about the camp and live upon its charity. He generously bade them welcome, though he feared a short supply of food ere he reached the sea.

One day Back was taking some observations with his astronomical instruments. Several of the Indians looked on with puzzled and anxious expressions of face, while they exchanged significant glances at each other, or muttered aside in low tones. They were evidently discussing the question of the probable use of the instruments.

At last they arrived at a conclusion quite satisfactory to themselves, but dangerous to the white stranger. The instruments were, they said, to raise the devil with, and they were, no doubt, the cause of the famine. Revenge, for such a calamity, was next in order in an Indian's mind. So Back's generous gifts of food came, in good time, to conciliate the fighting men.

The cloud which this condition of things gathered was silver-lined by the coming of Back's old friend, the chief Akaitcho. He led off in successful hunts. He scorned the suspicions which the instruments had inspired in his followers, and, in addressing Back, said: "The great chief trusts us, and it is better that ten Indians perish than that one white man perish through our negligence and breach of faith."

As the winter progressed, the cold, the stinted supply of food, and the desolation which everywhere prevailed, excited in the explorers a feeling of despondency. Even Back confesses that in spite of himself he at times felt his customary resolution falter.

Such was the state of heart at the camp April 23, made specially burdensome by a rumor that a favorite interpreter and guide of Back's former voyages had perished of hunger and cold in an attempt to visit him. While all were under these depressions a knock was heard at their cabin-door. Without waiting for the knock to be answered the stranger walked in and thrust a dispatch into the captain's hands, saying:—

"He returned, sir!"

"What! Augustus?" exclaimed Back. "Thank God!"

"Not Augustus, Captain Ross, sir; Captain Ross has returned!"

The news seemed too good to be true. But the dispatches told the story; they contained extracts from English papers affirming the joyous fact. Captain Back says: "In the fullness of our hearts we assembled together and humbly offered up our thanks to God for so wonderful a preservation."

The day was spent as a festival, and the gloom which had rested upon the camp was dissipated. Among the Indians who enlivened the camp by their presence was "Green Stockings," the "beauty" of her tribe, whom the reader may recollect as appearing in Franklin's narrative. She was now accompanied by a group of children, one, a babe, hiding away in her hood. When she was accosted by the pet name of her younger days she smiled, shook her head, and remarked, "I am an old woman now." But she was evidently pleased to have Back sketch her portrait.

In June the explorers started for Great Fish River. Though the search for Ross was happily ended, the captain desired to add something to the world's knowledge of the shores of the Polar Sea. A boat thirty feet long had been built. This they put on runners, for it was a long journey to the Fish River, through swamps and over lakes yet frozen. They reached it safely on the

28th of June. Here their valuable friends, M'Leod and Akaitcho, bid them farewell. The chief spoke despondingly of their enterprise. He said: "Indian don't know this river, and can't help you if you get into trouble. Esquimo live by the shore and will say, 'Peace, peace,' and strike you in the dark. I am afraid Akaitcho will never see the great chief again!" Thus warned Back started, a company of ten persons in all composing the expedition, and floated down the river. It proved to be a river extremely winding, full of rapids, whose rushing waters were thrown into sheets of foam by the numerous bowlders, and cataracts whose roar was at times heard several miles away. Its banks through its entire length, five hundred miles, were without a tree. Every-where nature seemed to have written the warning words, Man is not invited into these regions! But the explorers sailed on without the invitation, and in spite of the warning.

The half-breeds of the company were able canoe-men. They were born and trained in the midst of such wild scenes. Back says of one of them :—

"He ran our rickety and shattered canoe down four successive rapids, which, but for his skill, would have whirled it and every body in it to certain destruction. Nothing could exceed the self-possession and good judgment with which he guided the frail thing along the narrow line between the high waves of the torrent and the returning eddy. A foot in either direction would have been fatal; but with the most perfect ease, and, I may add, elegance and grace of action, his keen eye fixed upon the *run*, he kept her true to her course through all its rapid windings."

At another time they passed five rapids in a distance of three miles. They had scarcely taken breath on smoother sailing, before they were confronted by the most appalling one they had yet met with. The water, hemmed in by walls of ice, rushed through a narrow bed full of rocks. The Captain and Mr. King stepped ashore and mounted the high bank, while the half-breeds undertook the perilous voyage. Mr. King was farther down the stream than Back, and both were watching, with intense anxiety, the experiment. The lives of those ashore, as well as those in the canoe, were staked on its success. It shot safely, passed the captain, and was hid from his sight below Dr. King. The captain just then heard what sounded to his excited mind as a wild shriek! He saw King throw up his gun at the same time and rush forward. With an agitation more intense than he often felt, he followed the doctor. Having reached a point from which he could look beyond the rapid, he was relieved and gladdened by the sight of the boat in a quiet bay, and the crew safely landed. It was their wild whoop of triumph that he had heard.

On the 29th of July they came in sight of the highlands at the mouth of the river, and were soon on the shores of the chilling, frowning Arctic Sea. Less than two weeks' experience taught them the impossibility of unvailing the secrets of its shores. On the sea, successive masses of broken ice barred their progress. On land, they sunk knee deep in a slush of ice and snow. For ten days they had not a spark of fire, and, of course, neither warm food nor dry garments. Back, being a sensible as well as a brave man, wisely turned his face homeward. He had found the river, during his five hundred miles' voyage, expanding into five large lakes, rushing through rapids and pouring down cataracts, eighty-three in all. In the return trip these eighty-three descents in the river were to be passed by "portages," that is, by carrying on land the boat and its freight, often lifting both up craggy precipices. The voyage would have terrified many explorers into imbecility and failure. Back and his men accomplished it safely.

In September they went into winter-quarters at the old home at Fort Reliance, on Slave Lake. Here he found M'Leod and the faithful Akaitcho, who had made some most welcome preparations for their coming. Here, again, the hunt was begun, the schools put in operation, the Sabbath service observed, and the winter made as swift-footed as was possible to the slow-moving arctic months. It was the old experience of long, dark nights, cold, and dreariness.

Back arrived in England in September, 1835, having been absent a little more than two years and seven months.

He had not seen the North Pole, but his men

had picked up on the shore of the Polar Sea a piece of drift-wood nine feet long, which they declared was a part of it. This may have satisfied the ambition of the "rank and file" in respect to arctic discovery, considering how much of peril and suffering it cost, but it did not satisfy their leader. The next year, 1836, he was off again in the ship "Terror." This time he was to take Parry's route through Hudson Strait to Fury and Hecla Strait, examine the lower part of Prince Regent Inlet, enter Repulse Bay, and by sledges or ships, or by both boats and sledges, find his way to the coast of the Polar Sea, which he left about eighteen months before. Said those who sent him: "You can easily do this in one season, and so escape the arctic winter." A nice little plan! The scientific gentlemen at home would have done well, may be, at trying their hand at its execution.

The first thing King Ice did, even before the "Terror" reached Fury and Hecla Strait, was to frown upon it from a berg three hundred feet high; he then gave it a terrific shaking up in "a nip" between huge masses of ice. He next caught the ship in an icy cradle, gathered around her an immense floe, and rocked her about four months at will. No quiet rest for the winter in a chosen harbor was allowed. He toyed with her through the long season, from September to the summer of the next year, with malicious humor; now opening the floe and letting her down into the clear sea, then boxing her on one side with a crystal block, "like the side of a house," and giving her a buffet on the other by "a huge wave of hummocks." To vary the sport two floes were occasionally brought together, giving her agonizing "nips."* Finally, the "Terror," thoroughly terrified, was dismissed, the latter part of the summer of 1837, from his Ice Majesty's dominions, crippled and crestfallen. The profits of the expedition were a zero. But Back had done all that skill and courage could do, and he was rewarded by being made *Sir* George Back. He then rested from arctic labors.

* See Frontispiece.

CHAPTER XVII.

FRANKLIN MISSING: THE SEARCH COMMENCED.

WE are about to commence a sad era in the history of arctic explorations, or rather an era having its commencement and *stimulus* in a melancholy event, yet in its exhibition of heroism, and in the outlay of treasures and men to secure the results sought, surpassing all other eras. We shall endeavor to give its most striking features.

In 1844 Sir James C. Ross returned from the regions of the South Pole, having made a successful exploration in the ships "Erebus" and "Terror." The fever for more excursions to the North Pole broke out anew in England. These well-tried ships were docked, rejuvenated, equipped with all the skill which wealth could command and experience suggest, and put in command of the veteran officer, Sir John Franklin. He hoisted his flag on the "Erebus," and gave the command of the "Terror" to Captain Richard Crozier, a companion of Ross in the recent Antartic voyage. All the persons composing the exploration were one hundred and thirty-eight, every one tried, picked men. The transport "Daretto," under the command of Lieutenant Griffith, was laden with provisions, to be transferred to the ships in Davis Strait.

The instructions given to Sir John were somewhat in detail, yet left large discretion to his judgment, as determined by circumstance. The substance of the suggestions of the home authorities were these: He was to proceed with energy and directness through Lancaster Sound, to or as near Melville Island as possible the first season. Then came the old command, to push on to Bering Strait—if he could. It was only nine hundred miles! True, the greater part of that distance had been navigated, and the track mapped out by different men, including Franklin himself, starting at different times and from various points, such as Bering Strait itself, the mouth of the Mackenzie, and of the Coppermine River. But for one expedition to make a continuous push through the whole distance was quite another thing. But it was assumed that he would get through somehow, if not by a direct westerly or south-westerly course, by one north-westerly, up Wellington Channel. Having reached Bering Strait, the rest of his instructions could be easily followed. He was to sail to the Sandwich Islands and Panama, and send a special messenger with the good news.

All this planning was grandly comprehensive. It pleased Him by whom alone human devices come to pass to throw over the results, for many long, weary, and anxious years, a dark cloud. What appeared when it lifted we shall see.

The expedition sailed on the 19th of May, 1845. The "Daretto" gave the ships her supplies after reaching Davis Strait, according to the programme, and returned. The "Erebus" had five bullocks on board for fresh provisions in an emergency, and the whole stock of food was ample for three years. The explorers were seen on the 26th of July by the whaler "Prince of Wales," nearly in the middle of Baffin Bay, two hundred and ten miles from the entrance to Lancaster Sound, anchored to an iceberg, waiting the moving of the ice. Here the curtain drops.

Suspense concerning the fate of Franklin had grown painfully intense in the fall of 1847. Two years had passed without a word of information. The English Government planned immediately three searching expeditions, and they were sent into active service with all the dispatch consistent with thorough preparation. The first was to sail up the Pacific to Bering Strait and operate easternly. The second, under the eminent explorer Sir John Richardson, whom the reader has met before, was to go down the Mackenzie, and search along shore to the Coppermine. The third, under the popular J. C. Ross, was to penetrate Lancaster Sound, and find and follow Franklin's route. This last was on a grand scale, consisting of two fine ships, the "Enterprise" and "Investigator," each attended by small steam tow-boat "launches." All these were in operation in the early part of 1848. In the early fall of that year rumors through the whalers reached the home authorities concerning the plans of Ross which alarmed them. They regarded them as desperately brave. They at once sent the "North Star," supply ship, under the command of James Saunders, laden with provisions for Ross, and bearing specific orders. The "Star" was not to allow herself to be caught in the ice, but to return that season at all events, leaving at some well-known point her supplies if she did not find Ross. She did not overtake Ross, but did get caught and wintered in the ice.

All these explorations closed unsuccessfully toward the end of 1849.

The public mind was now continually stimulated in its interest concerning the lost ones. The veteran explorers—and they were many—as well as the veteran managers of explorations, came forward with their speculations and advice. Large rewards were promised, both by the Government and Lady Franklin, to excite the zeal of the whalers in making careful inquiry of the Esquimo, and in making diligent search along the shores, while pursuing their calling.

The Government, thus spurred on by its own desires and by public opinion, started three more expeditions in 1850. The first, in the tried vessels the "Enterprise" and "Navigator," supported by small crafts, were this time to start on the immediate search at Bering Strait, inasmuch as they did not get through from the other end. The second, under Dr. Rae, an old officer, was to try the Mackenzie and shore route. The third, a naval expedition, was to make another effort by way of Lancaster Sound, through which Franklin was supposed to have passed. Before we notice this squadron in detail, let us glance at certain non-official enterprises.

There was an expedition under the command of Captain Penny, an energetic, experienced commander of a whale ship. It consisted of a staunch ship, the "Lady Franklin," and a clipper-brig, the "Sophia." This expedition was prompted and mostly paid for by the devoted wife of Franklin.

In addition to Penny's vessels, Lady Franklin, out of her own purse, and with an exhaustive generosity, fitted out the "Prince Albert," a schooner-rigged craft of only ninety tons, but of faultless build.

Another expedition, under the veteran Sir John Ross, was equipped by public subscription, the Hudson Bay Company paying twenty-five hundred dollars. She sailed in June, 1850, a little later than the other vessels.

While England was thus stirring in the Christian work of saving the lost, the United States was not an idle spectator. Her naval ships, the "Advance" and "Rescue," we shall meet in the northern regions, and give them special notice in due time. These private enterprises were all destined for the regions beyond Lancaster Sound, and, as we shall see, met, and in a measure co-operated together.

The English naval squadron, consisting of the sailing vessels "Resolute" and "Assistance," rigged as barks, and two screw steamers, the "Pioneer" and "Intrepid," formed a searching expedition of peculiar interest. The steamers were tenders to the barks. Steam, as we have seen, had been tried before in the arctic service, but with no great success. In this case it was used on an ample scale, and with a skill and success resulting in part from the lessons of previous failures.

Having taken a look through the other vessels, we will lastly examine the "Pioneer," and take up our quarters for the voyage in her.

The "Resolute" was selected for the service because she was well built, and of the very best material. But a strong build for ordinary voyages was not considered sufficient for the boxing she was to receive in the regions of perpetual ice. She was strengthened with heavy timbers until her frame seemed the greater part of her. Ship architecture was sacrificed to ship endurance. Her bow became so broad that it resembled more that of a mud-scow than a sailing vessel, so that she pushed the water before her rather than sailed through it. An old "salt," who had been many times among the arctic floes and bergs, scorned the clumsy thing as he looked at her while she was in the dock-yard. "Lord, sir," he exclaimed, addressing his commanding officer, "you would think by the quantity of wood they are putting into them ships that the dock-yard maties believed they could stop the Almighty from moving the floes in Baffin Bay! Every pound of African oak they put into them the less likely they are to rise to pressure, and you must in the ice either rise or sink. If the floe cannot pass through the ship it will pass over it."

Internally the "Resolute" was arranged and equipped on the most generous scale for the safety and comfort of all on board. Hot air was distributed through the cabins and between the decks by an original and ingenious contrivance. Double defenses were made against the arctic cold. Ample and convenient cooking apparatus and apartments were provided. The mess-room of the crew was not neglected, but made both comfortable and inviting. A large captain's cabin gave him room for meetings of business, or social intercourse with the other officers; and the gun-room answered for the officers when they met together for their meals. The whole force of the "Resolute," officers and crew, consisted of sixty men. No expense or pains were spared to make this vessel equal in adaptation to her mission to any one which had ever sailed, and the "Assistance" was in every essential particular her equal. We have dwelt thus in detail on the description of the "Resolute" because of her marvelous later history. The reader will not forget her.

The *propellers* were each of four hundred tons burden, and were propelled by engines of sixty horse-power; they were rigged as three-masted schooners. Heavy extra planking was fastened securely to every part of both frame and decks, so that the sailors called them "bread-and-butter built." Their bows, made in a wedge form, were almost solid on the inside with oak and iron. The screw, stern-post, and rudder might be battered off by the ice, and yet the vessel made to swim. The internal accommodations were good, only that the heavy cargo of coal to drive the engines crowded Jack and the officers into close quarters. A sufficient quantity of this article was taken to enable them, with a consumption of seven tons a day, to tow the ships three thousand miles. If left without the burden of the sailing ship, they could steam five thousand miles. They carried about fifteen months' provisions. The crew of each steamer consisted of thirty men, all told.

The whole squadron was considered very smart —both men and vessels—and the enterprise was undertaken in the spirit of men who counted on taking the prize. It left England in the middle of the spring of 1850. It was under the command of Captain Austen, whose flag-ship was the "Resolute." Captain Ommaney commanded in the "Assistance," and Lieutenant Osborne in the "Pioneer," with whom, as we have stated, we are to deal, and Lieutenant Kater in the "Intrepid." For the sake of directness of statement we will use the first person.

On the 24th of June our squadron was in Baffin Bay, steaming north through an open sea, while the icebergs careered about us, some in solemn grandeur from their great size and compact make, and others almost ludicrous in their fantastic forms, etc.; all mingled together, and occasionally colliding in wild magnificence. "Hard a starboard! Steady! Port! port!" was shouted by the officer in command, and we flew past some huge crystal island against which the angry billows vainly dashed. The excitement was novel to some of us, and delightful to all. A storm soon came down upon us, yet we sped watchfully and fearlessly on :—

"And now there came both mist and snow,
And it grew wondrous cold ;
And ice, mast high, came floating by
As green as emerald.

"Through the drifts the snowy cliffs
Did send a dismal sheen ;
Nor shapes of men or beasts we ken—
The ice was all between.

"With sloping masts and dripping prow,
As who pursued with yell and blow,
Still treads the shadow of his foe,
And forward bends his head,
The ship drove fast, loud roared the blast,
And *northward* aye we fled."

Having hauled in for the land, we touched at the Danish settlement of Upernavik. We were soon off again and fell in with some whalers, and sighted Captain Penny's expedition—the "Lady Franklin" and the "Sophia." A storm being "in the wind," we made fast to an iceberg. This is done by sinking a heavy iron hook in the berg, to which a cable is attached. This is a risky way of anchoring. It may happen that the first blow that the sailor strikes, in order to settle the hook into the iceberg, rends the whole mass; or the part on which he stands may shelve off, and he be precipitated with it into the sea; or if the spot selected has not been carefully chosen to avoid such an accident, an overhanging piece of ice may, at the first stroke of his crowbar, fall upon his head. Even the ship itself may be injured by the disruption of the berg under these circumstances.

On this occasion we chose a berg one of whose sides sloped to the sea, having no overhanging points. The "Pioneer" and "Intrepid" were soon made fast to it, and we rode out the gale securely.

On the first of July the welcome signal came from the flag-ship: "Take the ships in tow." With a sixteen-inch hawser we took the "Resolute" by the nose. We were in company with Captain Penny's ships and several whalemen, but we soon left them astern. We dodged the bergs, pushed into an opening of the ice here, and made one in looser ice there, making headway through the loose pack as only propellers could. We were in the midst of scattered islands, from some of which the boats of the whalers were getting great quantities of eggs. After having for some time pushed our way through some rotten ice six inches thick, we came to a narrow lead of open water near the land and made fast for the night. Some of us climbed to the highest point of the near land to enjoy the profound silence of an arctic night. Of course our night was as the day, and we were restless and unable to sleep under the constant blaze of light. But birds and beasts had retired to rest with their wonted regularity, as if it was a night of darkness. A heavy bank of clouds about the sun and the subdued tints of the sky gave a pleasant quietude to the scene. Away westward, across Baffin Bay, the direction we would go, was ice, ice, ice. Now and then we could catch a glimpse of the windings of a narrow opening of clear sea. We will push through the windings on the morrow, we thought, and we shall see no more of the sailing vessels. But while we mused Penny's "Lady Franklin" and "Sophia" sped by. A breeze had sprung up, and the wide-awake Penny had spread his sails to it, and was beating the steamers. It would never do! We hurried on board, and, having had only a two hours' instead of a night's halt, we took the "Resolute" in tow and pushed forward. So much for the spur of a good example! The "Intrepid" followed, tugging the "Assistance." In the morning at seven o'clock we had passed Penny's squadron. After a tow of thirty hours a block of ice defied the butting of our sharp prows, and both steamers and the ships hauled up to convenient icebergs. The sea-fowl called loons were about us in countless numbers. Thousands could have been brought down by our guns if we had been disposed to devote ourselves for awhile to the sport. I climbed a small island near the "Pioneer." The only opening leading westward commenced astern of us.

Into this the provoking Penny was already entering, and was shooting ahead of our position. I amused myself in picking some anemones, poppies, and saxifras which grew in sheltered nooks. Though flowers of this rough arctic region, they possessed a delicate beauty.

When our vessels stopped, Captain Osborne sent the captain of the forecastle, with a boat's crew, to a headland not far off to get a supply of loons. The boat returned the next morning without having shot a single fowl, though not a man had a charge of powder or shot left. Captain Osborne called for the commander of the boat, and inquired how he managed to fire away one pound of powder and four of small shot and not bring home a loon. Hanging his head, like a school-boy caught robbing his seat-mate's dinner-basket, he answered :—

"If you please, sir, we fired it all into a bear!"

"What!" said the captain, "shot a bear with No. 4 shot!"

"Yes, sir; and if it hadn't have been for two or three who were afraid of him, we would have brought him aboard, too."

Sending the bear-hunting forecastle officer about his business with a reprimand for disobeying orders, the captain learned afterward the following facts: The boat's company, in passing a small island, saw a bear watching for his dinner at a seal-hole. They at once agreed that to be the first to bring a bear home would immortalize both them and their ship. They immediately poured into his broad sides showers of bird-shot! It probably made him feel a little uncomfortable and considerably vexed, especially at being molested while pursuing an honest business—that of getting a needed meal. He growled, snapped his teeth, and trotted round the island. The valiant hunters followed him, giving him more and more bird-shot. Not liking to be pestered in this way, bruin plunged into the water and swam to a piece of broken ice. The heroic hunters followed, and gave him a brass button and the blade of a knife, and the like missiles, which, in the absence of balls, they had crammed into their guns. They "made him jump," as "Old Abbot," the officer of the forecastle, declared, and as he reached the ice he was bleeding and torn, though not very seriously injured, for a polar bear can stand quite a quantity of bird-shot, besides several buttons and knife-blades. Abbot was after him, and as the bear attempted to get on the floe the battle was renewed. Old Abbot wanted bruin's skin, and bruin desired to keep it; and, besides, began to give signs, by earnest fighting, that he considered the joke carried far enough. The knights of the small-shot and boat-hooks were glad to retreat with their own skins, leaving bruin master of the field and four pounds of lead. But Old Abbot declared in the forecastle talk, that if he had been courageously sustained by his men the bear might have been brought to the ship, tamed, harnessed to a sledge, and made to save "an awful sight of hard dragging."

The reader must imagine us now, July 3, 1850, as

pushing up the eastern or Greenland side of Baffin Bay toward Cape York and Dudley Diggs, both of which may be easily found on the map. Our object was to get into the open water generally found on its northern boundary, and so cross to the eastern side and get into Lancaster Sound.

"The middle pack," as it was called, filled the center of the bay. Its eastern side was less frequently navigable than the western.

We started in the morning through a narrow in-shore "lead." We were soon beset with "bars" of ice with holes of water between them. The "Pioneer" undertook to break through the bars with its sharp prow, and then to drag the "Resolute" after it. We put on a full head of steam, and then rushed at it furiously. The ice thus smashed was pushed astern by the men, and a clear channel given us for another effort. We run astern far enough to get a good headway, set the propeller in motion, and came upon the bar again with a concussion which caused our vessel to quiver like a struck bullock. Fragments of ice flew like the spray, and great rents were made in it, and large cakes were broken off. But getting these cakes out so as to make a clear channel for another drive was a task which needed double our number of men. These could not be spared for the present from the other vessels, so, before our brave boys could get them out, they froze solid again! Not only so, but the icy *débris* about the "Pioneer" froze in the meantime, and the Frost King held us in his firm grip. Scores of strong men now came from the other vessels to help us. But it was too late! Ice tools—saws, chisels, iron-pointed poles, claws, and lines—were of no avail. We were unwillingly "docked," and had only to make the best of it, and wait for the fickle arctic thaws, winds, and currents to come to our aid and set us free.

CHAPTER XVIII.

STEAMING THROUGH ICE-FLOES.

WE were not disposed to improve the leisure of the "Pioneer's" confinement by repeating old Abbot's experiment of hunting polar bears with bird shot. But the following incident, taken from Captain Osborne's journal, shows that our sport was not without its excitement and danger:—

"A few birds flying about induced myself and some others to go out shooting, a foggy night promising to be favorable to our larders. The ice, however, was full of holes, and very decayed, in addition to which it was in rapid motion in many places from the action of wind and tide. The risk of such sporting was well evinced in my gallant friend M.'s case. He was on one side of a lane of water, and I on the other; a bird called the burgomaster flew over his head to the seaward, and he started in the direction it had gone. I and another shouted to warn him of the ice being in rapid motion and very thin. He halted for a moment and then ran on, leaping from piece to piece. The fog at this moment lifted a little, and most providentially so, for suddenly I saw M. make a leap and disappear. The ice had given way! He soon rose but without his gun, and I then saw him scramble upon a piece of ice, and on watching it, observed with a shudder that both he and it were drifting to the northward and away from us. Leaving my remaining companion to keep sight of M., and thus to point out the way on my return, I retraced my steps to the 'Pioneer,' and, with a couple of men, a hand-line, and boarding pikes, started off in the direction M. was in.

"I could tell my route pretty well by my companion's voice, which, in rich Milesian, was giving utterance to exclamations of the most original character: 'Keep up your courage, my boy! Why don't you come back? Faith, I suppose it's water that wont let you! There will be some one there directly! Hay! hay! hay! Don't be downhearted any way.'

"I laughed as I ran. My party placed themselves about ten yards apart, the last man carrying the line ready to heave in case of the leader breaking through. So weak was the ice that we had to keep at a sharp trot to prevent the weight of our bodies resting long on any one spot; and when we sighted our friend M., on his little piece of firm ice, the natural exclamation of one of my men was: 'I wonder how he ever reached it, sir!'

"M. assisted us to approach him by pointing out his own route, and by extending our line, and holding on to it, we at last got near enough to take him off the piece of detached ice on which he had providentially scrambled.

"I never think of the occurrence without a

sickening sensation, mixed with a comic recollection of my companion's ejaculations."

Our confinement was for only one day. Even before our captain's return with his half-frozen friend M., the turn of the tide gave evidence that the ice about the vessel was loosening and drifting away. They did not arrive a minute too soon. At noon of the next day we had the ships in tow, tugging away to the north-west. The fleet of whale ships, with all sails spread, showed an ambition to be up with us. Penny's ships were still ahead. We soon sighted the Devil's Thumb, a cape making the southern boundary of Melville Bay. It was an unattractive name given to a place of sad associations to sailors. Stormy winds blow here which have sunk many a noble craft. In one year twenty-eight whale ships went down before their terrific force.

We made good progress for two days, quite as long as good progress could be expected to continue in those regions. We had gone down to dinner with an intelligent captain of one of the whale ships. Our dinner and talk were abruptly broken off by an alarm from the deck. The face of the sky had vailed its smiles, and it was frowning terribly. A moaning gale, carrying before it a brown vapor, heralded the storm. The ice gleamed fiercely and the floes rapidly crowded together, as if to make a united attack on the ships, icebergs clashing in the mean time most savagely. Woe to the ships which came between them in their terrific assaults.

A scene of the most exciting interest now commenced. Suddenly the ice was peopled with five hundred men. Long saws, with every expedient known to arctic voyagers, were put in operation to open safe retreats in the solid ice, known as "docks," where the ships, each in his own cuddy, might be safe from the contending floes. Each crew worked as for his own life, as well as that of his vessel. Defiant songs from hoarse throats rose above the piping wind. Loud laughs and sharp witticism of the men mingled with the decisive orders of the officers. The ice was an average thickness of three feet. Saws ten feet in length were used. Huge blocks were cut out which were drilled, charged with powder, and blown to pieces, the officers doing this delicate part of the woık.

In an incredible short time explorers and whalemen were securely stowed away in a sound part of a floe, ready to go with it to any contest it might choose. The pressure of the whole pack was expended upon a chain of icebergs nearly ten miles north of our position. Floes charging icebergs was an unequal fight. Though every cubic yard of the solid ice which composed the floes weighed a ton, yet when hurled against the grounded bergs it was broken into fragments, thrown back, and piled into elevated heaps. The din of the battle was heard afar off.

A bear, snuffing, perhaps, the odors from our many camp fires, came in sight. Away scampered a multitude of hunters, rushing pell-mell at the game, armed with whatever first came to hand.

Bruin, alarmed in good time, and having a long start of his foes, might have won the race. But a sharp appetite, tempted by a seal which lay across his path, overcame his discretion. He stopped to eat, and that meal cost him his life. He was shot by the foremost hunters, and brought home in triumph.

The floes broke up as suddenly as they formed. Channels of water appeared in various directions. Through these the steamers towed the "Resolute" and "Assistance." The other sailing vessels were "tracted" along these channels, as in canals the boats are drawn by horses. The crews of the whale ships, often counting sixty men, were fastened to a long line by their "tract-belts," and, with shouts and songs, made their heavy ships plow through the water at good speed.

Frequent bars of thick ice brought to a standstill the sailing vessels, but we, with our powerful wedge-like prow, pushed by the giant engine, drove through them, dragging at our heels the "Resolute." The men from the whalers came quizzing round, wondering at our power; even Penny "gave it up," and rated steam a success in arctic navigation. Some of the whale ships, discouraged by this tedious way of making progress, turned back, though a few hung upon our rear.

The bars at last gave way, and Penny was the first to enter the clear sea. The "Pioneer" and "Intrepid" made the best speed they could with their awkward sailing charges. We could only sail three miles an hour thus encumbered. Alone we could have made five. Onward we steered, and we vainly imagined we should have no more ice-packs, but were soon to be in the "north water," and thence, sailing westward, to gain Lancaster Sound, and the region where we hoped to get upon the track of the lost Franklin. How this hope thrilled our hearts! But a few days only passed before all the searching squadrons were once more ice-bound. Between us and the shore was solid ice, called the land-floe, thirty miles in extent. It followed the irregularities of the coast, and seemed as firm as if it were an unchangeable part of it. Here and there, fast anchored within it, was a noble iceberg. We were held tight by the heavy, drifting ice, which, as it crowded against our ships, well deserved the name of "pack-ice;" at any rate we were packed into it very closely.

The glare of the sun so dazzled the eyes of the men as they walked about near the ship, that many ludicrous appearing spectacles were devised to screen the eyes, causing much merriment.

We were entertained too, as we sauntered about, by a beautiful refraction. Distant objects were lifted into the clouds and seen double. Some were curiously distorted. Captain Penny's ships, full thirty miles away, and whalers, lying in different directions, were brought into full view.

As the ice yielded to the current below, holes were opened. In these narwhal, or sea-unicorns, soon appeared, puffing and plunging about, seeming to be in fine spirits. An officer of the "Intrepid" fired at one of them, and, by special good luck, gave it a mortal wound. It was captured, dragged to the vessel, and great rejoicing made over it. Its flesh was repulsive in smell and taste, and not to our liking as food. Some of the men ate it with a relish, and declared it tasted like chesnuts! Just under the skin is a layer of fat or "blubber," which we carefully removed and boiled down to make oil.

The spiral horn protruding from the front of its head, was about five feet long, and the whole fish was nearly eleven feet long. We reckoned its size about an average. The horn had a blunt but polished point, the rest of it being covered with slime and a greenish sea-weed. The fishermen have various opinions about the use of this horn. It seems too clumsy as a weapon of attack or defense. Some think that he roots with it on the bottom of the sea, as a hog does in the sty. Others declare that they have seen him probe the fishes with it from the crevices of the ice, where they had hid to get out of his way. It must be quite handy for such a purpose. But as this tusk does not seem to be of very great use and is worn only by the male narwhal, it has been suggested that it is simply a badge of superior dignity. Baby narwhals wear two of these tusks, but one is deemed sufficient when they become grown folks.

We left the carcass of our specimen to be devoured by the sea-fowl, and the greediness with which great numbers of them feasted upon it, showed *their* opinion of narwhal flesh. The

Esquimo consider it good eating, and no doubt we should if very hungry. All agree that its flesh is an excellent preventive of the scurvy.

The good luck of the officer who shot it in securing a tusk to carry home as a trophy, caused the sport of these fish to be much disturbed. Showers of bullets were poured into them; and, if they could not dodge them they soon learned to be shy.

After refraction and the narwhals had, in turn, entertained us, a huge iceberg gave a rare exhibition for our gratification. We had noticed its great size and solidity. It looked sufficiently massive to defy the winter storms and summer thaws of centuries. All at once it began to fall to pieces, as if shaken by an earthquake. Large masses fell from it into the water, shattered into a thousand pieces! The sea around it seethed like a caldron. The swell that it occasioned lifted the floes for ten miles. We were glad that its dissolution took place at a safe distance from us.

One day Captain Penny, being on board of us, went into the "crow's nest," and swept the horizon with his glass. Hurrying to the deck and making preparations for a hasty departure for his own vessel, he exclaimed: "The land ice is breaking up!" We knew that his keen and practiced eye could not be deceived, and that ten miles of icy girding of the shore was soon to be in motion, threatening destruction to whatever came within its powerful "nips." We instantly armed for the conflict, and every man was at his post of duty, awaiting the onset. Soon it came. Every timber and plank cracked and groaned, the treenails and iron bolts snapped with sharp reports, and the vessel was lifted bodily and considerably thrown over on her side; the deck arched with the pressure on her side, the bulk-head even cracked, and the whole noble craft was wrung with a quiver of agony. The floe held us in its giant grip, and, as if intent upon our destruction, piled up as high as the bulwarks.

The men, without orders, but by a general impulse, packed up their clothes, and other little property, and brought them upon deck. They were ready for the desperate scramble for life upon the ice, when the fatal crisis of the "Pioneer" came. They stood in knots waiting for orders, while officers with anxious eyes watched the floe edge as it harshly ground against the sides, to see if the strain was lessening. Suddenly the writhing vessel, like a deer loosened from the deadly coils of an anaconda, settled back into a natural position. We were safe! But a deep scar on her side forty feet long, and twenty-one broken timbers upon one side, bore witness to the severity of her trial.

For eleven days we struggled in this pack. But our great deliverance from imminent death gave us hope for the future. Surely the Divine hand upheld us, and we shall not fall in coming perils. So we felt. The men shouted and sung while at their exhausting work. Sometimes roars of laughter evinced their unflinching courage. Men and officers shared alike in labor and peril, and rejoiced together; both hove at the capstan, and dragged at the tract-line. The dignity of the quarter-deck was laid aside as useless; Jack, feeling the responsibility of the hour, took no advantage of the familiarity of his superiors, but played the part of a man.

When the giant of the north bid us stop, we had our sports upon the ice. No school-boys ever played heartier. Men of gray hairs mingled with the youngest in the plays of youth. The panting, running, leaping, clapping of hands, roars of laughter, shouts of "There now, that's not fair; run again," and uproarious exclamations of triumph, all declared we were boys again.

While the crowd was thus employed, a few were quietly pitching quoits. A still smaller number strolled off, and, may be, talked of the past and sagely discussed the future.

We occasionally had a bear chase by way of variety. Bruin was keen on the scent, and had a tough hide, which, though not ball proof, enabled him to carry off many with impunity. He could endure, too, long teasing and many thrusts from our pikes. But his skin was in great danger when a troop of our "boys" went shouting after him. We always pitied, but always killed him when we could. The way he sometimes showed his teeth at us gave stimulating assurance that he had the will to kill us without the pity.

The early part of August, 1850, found us once more afloat in tolerably clear water. The squadron having separated when drifting in the floes, a vexatious delay occurred to enable all the vessels to come together again.

While thus waiting we saw in the hazy distance a schooner with two smaller crafts in attendance. They hung upon our rear for several days before we could make out what they were. On closing up they proved to be the "Felix," a searching vessel, commanded by the veteran explorer, Sir John Ross, with a small sailing-boat towing astern, and the "Prince Albert," in charge of Commander Forsyth. Their news from England was joyfully received, it being a month later than our own. All our friends were well and all hopeful of our success. We put these last letters from home away to read and reread in the dark, long arctic winter, when, may be, clouds might be darkening our prospects of ever seeing again the loved ones who wrote them.

Our course was now one through alternate floes and open water. On the ninth of August Captain Penny slipped into a narrow lane of water and shot ahead of our squadron, and the new comers did the same. The steamers themselves seemed to resent this dropping into the stern chase. Three weary days had they chaffed behind a barrier of ice two or three hundred yards broad and three feet thick. They could endure it no longer, and they addressed themselves to the work of its destruction. Its weakest part was carefully studied. The incumbrance of the ships was for the time shaken off. The larger part of the crews were sent to the place of attack, with short hand-lines, claws, iron bars, chisels, and various other tools. Some of the officers accompanied them with gunpowder.

All being ready, the propellers, in turn, drew back, and, with a full head of steam, rushed at the floe. The wedge-bow penetrated, crushing many tons and cracking the ice in every direction. The crushed portions floated away of themselves. The cracked and loosened parts were immediately manned by the blue jackets with long lines in hand; men on the bows of the steamer held the other end of this line, she shot astern, carrying great rafts of ice, and the jolly men who were upon them. When one steamer went thus astern, the other dashed into the breach. The gun-powder, the while, dealt the icy barrier hard blows. The scene was exciting, and the blood warmed in our veins in spite of arctic cold. The enemy surrendered at discretion, and the next morning we were steaming joyously on after the Ross and Penny squadrons, dragging our clumsy ships at our heels. Myriads of birds crossed our track, so stupidly tame that we might have taken tons of them.

Our steamers soon caught up with the "Felix" and the "Prince Albert," and avenged themselves of the late stern chase by taking them both in tow.

August 13th we were steaming under Cape York; Melville Bay was passed; its turbulent waters and icy barriers were conquered; "large waters" stretched away to the west and invited us on our desired course. The "Assistance" and "Intrepid" paused at Cape York to communicate with the natives, while our steamer pushed on. We passed Penny, who, though he knew the "Felix" had letters for him from home, held steadfastly on his course, with characteristic pluck.

In the evening the "Intrepid" overtook us with orders to turn back. Important information, it was said, had been obtained of an Esquimo concerning the fate of Franklin. The "Intrepid," having left us this order, pushed on after Penny to get his well-tried Danish interpreter, Mr. Petersen. Incredulous as to the story of the Esquimo, we reluctantly turned our prow from the coveted western shores of Baffin Bay.

CHAPTER XIX.

SIGNIFICANT RELICS.

THE story, on account of which the exploring fleet was detained, was repeated on the deck of the "Pioneer." The relator was Adam Beck, a South Greenland Esquimo, who had received from the white settlements what civilization he had. His story, in brief, was this: That two ships were crushed in the ice a little north of Cape York, where we now were, in 1846; some of their men wore epaulets; the entire crew were soon after murdered by the natives.

Mr. Petersen, the Danish interpreter, regarded the whole story as a pure fiction, and charged Beck with lying, in the expectation that his story would induce some of the ships to return, and he by this means get a passage to South Greenland. An Esquimo lately taken on board our steamer took the same view. We, of the "Pioneer," regarded Beck as a liar. But Sir John Ross, of the "Felix," gave some credit to the story, so our commander, Austin, sent the "Assistance" and "Intrepid" to make further inquiry about the region named as the scene of the wrecks and murder; they were also to ascertain the fact about a ship which the natives agreed had wintered safely in that region the last season. This ship proved to be the "North

Star." Having done this errand, the "Assistance" and "Intrepid" were to cross to the west side, and examine the north shore of Lancaster Sound.

On the 15th of August we, the "Pioneer," with the "Resolute" and "Prince Albert" in tow, gladly started again westward. After four hours of the old experience with the ice-pack, we reached the western waters. For forty-seven days we had been in almost perpetual conflict with ice. It had beset us behind and before. In calm and storm, by day and night, whether we slept or woke, off or on our guard, it never left us, except for a brief moment, that it might gather strength for a fiercer attack. Such had been Melville Bay. But here was nothing except water! How beautiful! Even the great giants of the north, the icebergs, watchful sentinels of the regions of cold, only seldom showed here their majestic forms. We turned our bows south-west, and steamed on both night and day. Our only annoyance was a dismal fog, but through it we steered. At one time, a spanking breeze starting up, the "Resolute," setting all sail, took our steamer in tow, and for four hours returned our favor, in part, of long and weary hours of towing. It was a capital joke, and we enjoyed it.

We were soon at the mouth of Lancaster Sound, where we dropped the "Prince Albert," to proceed to Regent Inlet, while we explored for awhile a little further south.

On the 26th of August, after days of a calm sea, we were running from the north side of Lancaster

Sound, toward the south-west, across the entrance to Regent Inlet, toward Leopold Island. A piping breeze was after us, giving assurance of an arctic gale. Ahead Cape York gleamed luridly through an angry sky, while the falling mercury warned us that the clear sea, with which we cared not for the tempest, might at any time give place to our old enemy, the floes. The "Pioneer" rolled and pitched like a sea-monster in mental agony, and refused all the devices of her staggering officers to comfort her. About half-past one in the morning the lifting of an angry sky gave us glimpses, through snow and squalls, of a precipitous coast not far ahead of us. Increasing daylight showed us an intervening pack, along whose edge the gale made the sea boil, and sent over it clouds of spray. It was a wild, terrific sight, and would have been a scene to enjoy but for the serious work it was likely to give us. It wore away to the north. Toward the close of the day we were not far from Beechey Island, near the mouth of Wellington Channel. We were having nights now that were not all daylight, and the welcome moon shone beautifully as the sun dipped behind North Devon. While we were admiring the scene the man at the mast-head startled us with the shout, "A sail!" It proved to be Penny's "Sophia." Yes, Captain Penny was at hand as usual. Two officers came on board, and gave us the following welcome intelligence:—

The "Intrepid" and "Assurance" had cruised about the locality where, according to Adam Beck's story, two ships had, in 1846, been crushed. But they found nothing, either in relics or the talk of the natives, to confirm the tale. They had ascertained, however, that the exploring vessel, the "North Star," had spent comfortably the last winter there. But since following us into Lancaster Sound their searching had been well repaid. They had found at Cape Riley, the eastern land-side of the mouth of Wellington Channel, numerous traces of a visit from English seamen. Bits of rope, broken bottles, a part of a deep-sea rake, and the various marks of an encampment, were scattered here and there.

Having found these stimulating relics, a boat-load of officers and men visited Beechey Island, lying just a little seaward of the cape. They picked up on the shore more relics of English visitors. Looking sharply about they observed upon a cliff, which rose sharply from the beach, a cairn—a rounded heap of stones. With almost breathless haste and deep solicitude they ascended the cliff and removed the stones carefully, one by one. But no word of writing or further clew to the identity of those raising the cairn was found. While standing with disappointed-looking faces about the upturned foundation of the monumental pile, they saw with alarm a hungry polar bear trotting boldly toward the two men left in charge of the boat. None of the party had brought arms of any kind from the vessel. Here was a fix! The men launched the boat and rowed in haste to the steamer. Bruin gave chase. Now what if he turns back and attacks the unarmed party on the island! He seemed, before giving chase, to have deliberately surveyed the whole party, both those on the hill as well as the men in the boat, and to comprehend the situation. But he scorned to attack the defenseless; or, perhaps, he had heard rumors of these strangers which led him to think that it was wisdom to give them a wide berth. He followed the boat a rod or two, turned off and swam for the ice-pack, on which he soon disappeared. We think there were no more *unarmed* visitors on the island during the season.

Captain Penny having heard of these traces, as all believed, of Sir John Franklin, returned to his own ship, as he declared, "to take up the search from Cape Riley like a blood-hound." This he did with good results. He soon reported that another camping-ground was discovered. The tent-floor was neatly paved with stones. Bird bones were strewn around, and remnants of meat-canisters found of unmistakable English make.

The American Grinnell Expedition, in the "Advance" and "Rescue," on the same errand as ourselves, under the command of Lieutenant De Haven, was now joined with our squadrons in the exciting search. The shores of the entire vicinity, in a sweep of many miles, were likely to be closely examined. Here were now our four vessels, Penny's two, Sir John Ross's "Felix" and her tender, the "Mary," and the American "Advance" and "Rescue." Penny, as usual, was in luck, and soon found evidence of more tent-encampments. But, as he was carefully examining one day the southern slope of Beechey Island, he found a large number of preserved meat-tins. A rounded pile of these, filled with sand, was discovered on the top of the slope; but a careful removal of these, can by can, revealed no documents.

Beyond these, and farther north, were still more important relics. The site of a carpenter's shop, an armorer's working place, washing-tubs, coal-bags, pieces of old clothing and rope; and, lastly, the decisive evidence of the English visitors, three graves. These were scrupulously neat, like all the graves of Englishmen, even of the poor, whether in the rural cemeteries at home or on foreign shores. The inscriptions contained no inflated verse. They were as follows:—

"Sacred to the memory of J. Torrinton, who departed this life January 1, 1846, on board H. M. S. 'Terror,' aged 20 years."

"Sacred to the memory of Wm. Braine, R. N., of H. M. S. 'Erebus;' died April 3, 1846, aged 32."

"'Choose you this day whom ye will serve.' Joshua xxiv, 15."

"Sacred to the memory of J. Hartwell, A. B., of H. M. S. 'Erebus,' died January 4, 1846, aged 25 years."

"'Thus saith the Lord of hosts; Consider your ways.' Haggai i, 7."

Here then, at last, was decisive proof that Franklin's ships were not crushed by the ice in Baffin Bay, nor the men murdered by the natives. Thus far we were on the right track. Now, if in some of the monuments of stone, such as we had discovered, put up beyond a doubt by the men of the "Erebus" and "Terror," we could find a document left by Franklin, telling us the route taken by him after leaving Beechey Island, all the exploring squadrons would joyfully face any danger in following him. To find such a record now engaged the attention of every ship's company. Much additional evidence was obtained that he had made Beechey Island his first winter-quarters; but no documents were found.

Winter was now well upon us. The American vessels took a courteous leave of us, and bore away, as they had been ordered, for New York. By the middle of September our squadron were caught in a floe, a mile from Griffith Island, the nearest land, where we were obliged to make a stop for the winter. Captain Penny and Sir John Ross, with their vessels, had chosen snug winter retreats twenty miles from us, near Beechey Island.

It was arranged for the three squadrons to take three different routes in the spring: one to the north-west, up Wellington Channel; one west, past if possible Melville Island; and the third south-west, beyond Cape Walker, along the western shore of Boothia. During October parties were sent out as far as possible in these directions to make deposits of provisions, securing them from the bears' sharp teeth and strong paws by heaps of stones.

One of these parties were saved from a plunge into the water, if not from drowning, by the sagacity of a shaggy polar who was at the time on a hunting excursion. The officer in charge had not noticed that he was getting on newly formed and weak ice. Just ahead was bruin cautiously feeling his way along by stopping occasionally and jumping upon the ice to try its strength. The explorers took the hint of caution and soon found reason to do so. We are sorry to record that they shot their good adviser, and subsequently dragged him to the ship for dog food.

One illustration of our manner of camping on these excursions will answer to show their general character.

There are seven of us, officers and men; common labor and peril pretty much removing official distinction. It is an October evening. One almost unbroken mantle of white covers sea and land. It is a dreary monotony, and all nature seems to shiver in the frosty atmosphere. We make a "soft spot," by clearing away the larger pieces of limestone, and arranging the smaller pieces into something like a floor of paved work. We erect our brown Holland tent over this. One of us is cook for the day, aided by one who will be cook to-morrow. The cooking apparatus is a boats' stove, eighteen inches long and nine broad, in which *lignum vitæ* is used as fuel. Water is obtained by melting the snow, and then the boiling and cooking is done in the open air, and so supper is not hurried up with boarding-house promptness.

While two are thus employed, others take guns and try their luck in securing fresh provisions. Bear meat is not sought after just now, and the animal under whose skin such meat grows has liberty to keep both his skin and flesh and give our camp a wide berth.

The hunters having returned, the cook reports,—"Supper is ready, sir." It is a *pemmican* supper! It is *supposed* to be made of the best rump-steaks and suet, worth a shilling and six-pence a pound. Our men generally vote it composed of worn-out horses and Russia tallow. It is not sweet in savor, though strong in nourishment. To the dainty it is nauseous, but to an arctic appetite, especially to those making, as we propose to do, sledge-journeys of four or five hundred continuous miles, it is a delicious morsel. A "jolly hot basin of tea," with biscuit to crumb into it, and our dish is fit "to set before the queen."

Supper being done, the tent is carefully swept, and the pebbles which compose our bed are re-arranged. We call this last operation—"Stirring up the feathers." A waterproof blanket is thrown over these to prevent the moisture which the warmth of our bodies raises from the frosty "feathers" from wetting us through. Boots and jackets are taken off and used for pillows. Then we all, except the cook, draw our legs and bodies into blanket-bags, roll ourselves up in wolf-skin robes, and, our prayers being said, we are about ready to compose ourselves to sleep. But while the cook is "clearing up," getting ready the breakfast for cooking, fastening down the tent, and seeing that every thing is in order, many a tough yarn is told, and laughter-exciting joke made. After a while the cook, having "tucked us in," shouts—"All right!" Then we, seven jolly explorers, lying alternately head and feet across the tent, "cuddle down" and sleep; yes, *sleep* soundly, with the thermometer outside 30° below zero.

An arctic winter was now, November 8, fairly upon us. We obtained to-day the last glimpse of the sun. Two of us went upon the heights of Griffith Island at mid-day, and saw his pleasant face, though he was in fact seventeen miles below the horizon. We were indebted to refraction for this last adieu from the King of Day. However hopeful of the future we might be, and possessed as we certainly were with more occasion for courage than most other sojourners in the long arctic night, the bravest needed to stay his mind upon God. This, we trust, many at least of our company felt. The religious services of our vessel had a more solemn meaning. The prayers were deeper toned. The following form of supplication, written for us before we left England, and included among the thoughtful presents of kind friends, was used with profit:—

"O Lord, our Heavenly Father, who teachest man knowledge, and givest skill and power to accomplish his designs, we desire continually to wait, and call, and depend upon thee. Thy way is in the sea, and thy paths in the great waters. Thou rulest and commandest all things. We therefore draw nigh unto thee for help in the great work which we now have to do.

"Leave us not, we beseech thee, to our own

counsel, nor to the imaginations of our foolish and deceitful hearts; but lead us by the way wherein we should go. Do thou, O Lord, make our way prosperous, and give us good success. Bring all needful things to our remembrance; and where we have not the presence of mind, nor the ability, to perform thy will, magnify thy power in our weakness. Let thy good providence be our aid and protection, and thy Holy Spirit our Guide and Comforter. Endue us with such strength and patience as may carry us through every toil and danger, whether by sea or land; and, if it be thy good pleasure, vouchsafe to us a safe return to our families and homes.

"Bless us all with thy favor, which is life, and with all spiritual blessings in Christ Jesus; and grant us so to pass the waves of this troublesome world, that finally we may come unto thine everlasting kingdom. Grant this for thy dear Son's sake, Jesus Christ our Lord. Amen."

A glance at our good ship, inside and out, and at what is going on in and around her, may interest the reader: Our upper decks are now cleared of all the lumber and covered in; boats secured on the ice; the warming apparatus set at work; masts and yards made as snug as possible; rows of posts set up to show the road in the darkness and snow-storms, from ship to ship; hole cut in the ice, to be kept always open, for a supply of water in case of fire, and a winter round of duties entered upon to keep up the discipline, cheerfulness, and health of the men.

This work being done—the *real* work was easily and soon done—the men found pleasure and healthful employment in renewing the sports of boyhood. They built snow walls, houses, and forts, such as all boys in the lands where snow is found have delighted to build. They cut out of the snow obelisks, sphinxes, vases, and cannon. These were sometimes carved with taste and skill, and gave the floes a picturesque appearance. But their greatest triumph in snow sculpture was in the statue of Britannia. Its stately form, looking west, was admired by all.

These out-door amusements were, of course, only for awhile. When they failed the wits and tact of the officers were drawn out to keep every mind healthfully exercised. Schools, religious services, newspapers—one an illustrated sheet—a club-room, a saloon, dramatic performances, mask balls, and instructive lectures—all claimed a share of attention. Artists and musicians, orators and teachers, common laborers and professional men, were all represented in this routine of instruction and amusement. Men gifted in telling the stories of the "olden times," especially if they could repeat the tales concerning early arctic heroes, were always sure of an attentive audience.

It is a day of total darkness so far as the sun is concerned, but the manner in which it is spent fitly represents the average of our winter days. Let us step below. The lower deck and cabins are lighted with candles and lamps. No external air is admitted except that which is under control as it passes in through pipes and passes out through ventilators. Double doors are carefully adjusted to prevent draughts. It is breakfast-time. Reeking hot cocoa steams on every mess-table. We are not on "short rations," and a hearty meal is eaten. This done, a few remain below to clear up and arrange for dinner; the rest pull on warm clothes and go on deck. Here, after the domestic work below is done, all hands are mustered. The officers inspect the men to see if they are clean, watching sharply every occasion of disease. The ship is then examined to see if every part is clean, and all hands disperse to their petty labor, and then amuse themselves according to their several tastes. The upper deck being covered, as we have stated, is kept clear for gymnastic exercises. If the wind is not violent a few venture to stroll away from the ship on the ice.

At noon the seamen dine on soups, and preserved meats called by them "salt horse." The officers dine later on fare not essentially different. The resources of the men in inventing entertainment flags a little in the afternoon, and the evening meal with hot tea comes to break the monotony. It is school night, and the pupils go to their self-imposed tasks, and the teachers to their gratuitous service. Bookish men con over some interesting volume. Artists are sketching or painting by candle-light, and men given to the use of the pen are writing up their journals, or putting on paper thoughts born under the inspiration of arctic skies.

Music, chess, and cards receive their share of attention, while social conversation is seldom wanting in vivacity; and, since we unfortunately have not learned the better way, cigars, pipes, and grog bring round the bed-time.

But in spite of all our amusements, labor, study, conversation, and earnestly-cultivated heroic bravery of which we boasted, there was a very noticeable tendency among us to talk of England, friends, and home.

While the above methods of passing the time occupied the attention generally, there were some who devoted all their energies to render successful the object of our search. They were practicing the various ingenious means, put into our hands before we left home, of communicating with the lost ones. Rockets in the calm evenings glowed and flashed along the sky, and were responded to by Penny's ships, though we were twenty miles apart.

We employed balloons in a novel way. Those of oil-silk, capable when inflated of raising a pound, were used. When one was all ready to ascend, a piece of slow match five feet long was attached. Along this match-rope, at short intervals, pieces of colored silk and paper were secured with thread; on them were printed information of our present position and intended lines of search in the spring. The balloons, when liberated, rose and sailed away, dropping the glaring messages on the white snow as the match burned. Our silent prayers followed them that they might fall under the eye of some one belonging to the lost ships. Great care was used to send them up when the wind promised to carry them to the north and north-west.

A few fire-balloons were also sent up.

It was vexatious to see these aerial vessels sail about in the upper currents of air in the most fickle manner. Starting off north-west, they were soon gliding away to the south-east, altering their course several times before disappearing from sight.

The greatest distance at which we found any of these pieces of silk or paper was fifty miles. Some may have gone many times as far.

Another means of communication used were carrier-pigeons. We of the "Pioneer" brought out none of them, and we confess that we were inclined to laugh at the idea of these birds being able to reach their far-away home in safety if dispatched from any of our exploring ships; but there were four of them on board the "Felix," given to Sir John Ross by a lady friend living near Ayr, in Scotland. He agreed to set two of them at liberty when he went into winter-quarters, and the other two when Sir John Franklin was found. On the 7th of October, 1850, when snugly tucked away in his harbor, near Beechey Island, he sent off the youngest couple. They were put into a basket attached to a balloon, a slow match being so arranged as to liberate and launch them into the air, to commence their flight at the expiration of twenty-four hours. The balloon ascended to commence its aerial voyage when it was supposed that the atmospheric current would bear it many miles their way. It blew a gale at the time and the temperature was below zero. In about five days one of them, as the lady owner affirmed, reached the dove-cot where it was born. It had disencumbered itself somehow of the message with which it was intrusted, though its feathers bore evidence of its having started with one. The distance in an air line was not less than twenty-four hundred miles; the distance which the balloon had borne it we, of course, cannot tell, but its sustained flight on the wing must have been truly wonderful.

The experiments we made to use kites as signals to parties at a distance were not very successful; but we used them to good purpose. When our sledges were running before a strong wind on level and smooth ice we let fly the kites as sails, and with shouts and laughter sped on our way. But, of course, we could not often have smooth sailing and a fair breeze, so that for the greater part of the time the sails were a dead weight on us.

There was among us another device for conveying intelligence to our lost friends, though it must be confessed we adopted it more for amusement than in confidence of its success. Curious little arctic foxes were slyly peering about our ships. Some of these we caught, fixed a brass collar on them, on which our message was engraved, and then set them free. The discharge of one of these foxy postmen was a signal of a general chase by officers and men, with bursts of laughter and wild shouts which, at times, seemed so to bewilder them that they ran hither and thither, making their capture easy if we had desired it. A more courteous dismissal would, we think, have better disposed them to a faithful delivery of our messages.

These liberated foxes were presumed to immigrate to distant and more friendly neighborhoods after this rough experience. But it leaked out that the "men" in the forecastle were nightly recapturing these collared gentlemen, making dainty meals of their flesh, and packing away their skins for future speculations with fur-dealers. Orders were promptly issued that foxes taken alive must be liberated. Jack, from the going forth of this edict, took good care that all foxes putting their noses into the traps should be found dead. The fact seemed to be that these cunning animals liked the fare they scented and occasionally tasted about our ships, and were willing to risk their lives in getting a second taste; they seemed in nowise inclined to do our errands to our lost friends.

The dark winter passed thus away. On the 7th of February, 1851, a man at the mast-head proclaimed the good news that the sun had returned. The rigging of all the vessels was soon manned to get a glimpse of his welcome face. He had been absent three months. He was greeted with prolonged and hearty cheers. For one whole hour he blessed us by his presence and then retired, promising us a longer stay each successive day until he should pay us the long summer visit.

Preparations were now hurried forward for the

proposed sledging. Time flew on rapid wings, and April was upon us before we were fully ready for it. Five hundred men, British and Americans, were astir within the frigid zone, aiming at the same result—that of saving Sir John Franklin.

The men of our squadron were mustered, on the 12th of April, under a projecting point of Griffith Island, to be inspected by our chief. This done, we returned to our ship and spent the Sabbath quietly, having religious service, and indulging some sober though not depressed feelings in reference to the responsible and laborious duties which we were to enter upon on Monday. But that day came breezy with blinding snow. Tuesday evening came with abated wind, and the thermometer *only* fourteen degrees below zero, so we donned our traveling gear, harnessed ourselves to the sledges, listened to a brief but earnest prayer, in which we were commended to God's providential care, and started.

We will not detain the reader with the details of our desperate struggles over hummocks, our sufferings from snow blindness and frost bites, and our varied perils and the unflinching bravery of our men for fifty-eight days. Our return journey was five hundred miles in a direct line. The last day homeward we made twenty-five miles. This may attest the pluck with which we closed our search. The other sledge parties returned soon after. Only one man had fallen, and he faltered at the beginning. No additional information concerning Sir John had been obtained. Penny's sledge parties to the north-west had been equally unsuccessful. No news of the lost ones came from any exploring party, though thousands of miles had been traversed to secure it.

Our icy fetters having fallen off on the 11th of August, the steamers took their ships in tow and once more pushed out of Lancaster Sound. Captain Penny's ships left for England at the same time, and Sir John Ross was homeward bound. Our squadron spent a few weeks in vain search further north, when we, too, squared away for "home, sweet home."

CHAPTER XX.

YANKEE ICE-FIGHTING.

WE have referred to the fact that the people and Government of the United States were not idle spectators of the efforts of England to save her lost explorers. The American interest in the searching expeditions sent out in 1848 from England was preparing the public mind for one which should fly the stars and stripes. To prompt this interest, Lady Franklin wrote to the President. Through him she called upon us, "as a kindred people, to join heart and hand in the enterprise of snatching the lost navigators from a dreary grave."

Congress moved in the matter, but with a tardiness which belongs to "great bodies." Delay in this business was the assurance of failure, so that the coming forward just in time of a princely merchant of New York, tendering a part of the resources of his purse, saved probably the credit of our nation in reference to the arctic search. Mr. Henry Grinnell fitted out two of his vessels, and gave them for the enterprise to the Government. The President, under the authority of Congress, detailed from the navy such officers and seamen to man them as he deemed competent to the service, and as had also an ambition for the perilous undertaking. The vessels received the appropriate names of "Advance" and "Rescue." They were small brigs, both together rating only two hundred and thirty-five tons. They were simply lumbering coasters to the eye, but, judged by their adaptation to the service to which they had been appointed, brave looking crafts. Their hulls had two coverings, each, of two and a half inch oak plank; a heavy shield of strips of sheet-iron extended from the bows along the sides. Their decks were double, and made water-tight. The inside was ceiled with cork, to secure greater warmth and dryness. Their wooden frame-works were made doubly strong. The rudders could be unshipped and taken on board in four minutes. Neither careful planning, skill, nor expenditure of money were wanting to make them all they needed to be.

The crews were man-of-war's men, of various nationalities, constitutions, and habits, and were not especially promising in their make-up, but proved true under severe tests—a fact creditable, we should think, to the officers, as well as men. The larger vessel, the "Advance," carried thirteen seamen and four officers; the "Rescue" had the same number of officers, and twelve seamen.

The expedition was commanded by Captain De Haven, in the "Advance," under whom was Lieutenant Griffin, in the "Rescue." Elisha K. Kane, M.D., who rose to such distinction among arctic navigators, and to whose ready pen we are indebted for rich stores of information of the northern seas, was the surgeon of the flag-ship, "Advance."

After all that was done to make the outfit thorough, the comforts and aids in prosecuting the search on the part of the American vessels compared poorly with those of the steam-propeller squadron we have just described. The cabins were of small dimensions, containing just four not roomy berths. Jack's quarters were, of course, crowded. The smashing of floes was to be done by the brigs themselves, without the powerful aid of the giant steam-engine.

The squadron started on its errand of love on the 23d of May, 1850. The witnessing crowd waved them kind adieus from the wharves and house-tops, and many a "God bless you!" was breathed as the news of their departure was read in the households of the land, while many hearts in the fatherland were thrilled with joy at their noble purpose.

We shall assume a cozy place in the cabin of the flag-ship, where we hope to be no intruder, while we carefully note the events more or less peculiar to this expedition.

On the 17th of June the night left us, or rather the darkness, for our sun, having retired at the unseasonable hour of ten P.M., rose at the early hour of two A.M. We learned by the nerve-disturbing continuance of blazing light how blessed is darkness to the heavy eyelids.

We were, in a few more days' sail, well into the region of icebergs and glaciers, and the rugged, ice-bound and snow-clad shore of Greenland came into view. A solitary berg, of majestic proportions, attracted our attention. Behind it the sun was shining, lighting the sea with a crimson hue. While we were watching the berg it lost its balance, probably by the shelving off of some projecting crag, and it began to swing back and forth, rolling vast waves in a widening circuit over the sea. This sudden action of the berg startled from their resting-place in its icy crevices myriads of birds, which rose in a dark, circling cloud above it. The scene was novel to us and impressive.

On the 24th of June our sun, having descended to the verge of the horizon, started again on its upward course.

We were soon at a Danish port in the Bay of Disco. Here we learned that the English squadron, under Commodore Austin, had left only the day before. His steamers, the "Pioneer" and "Intrepid," would keep him, we thought, in advance of our clumsy sailing vessels.

While we waited on deck for our boat to be manned to carry us ashore we observed a black object in the water coming from the land toward the ship. It moved rapidly and seemed like a Newfoundland dog. As it approached we could discern a black projection from it too long for the neck and head of a dog; while a curious flapping was going on, first on this side and then on that, as it sped swiftly along. When in a few moments it was along side, we obtained our first clear view of a Greenland kayak. It was canoe-shaped, and over its frame seal skins were tightly drawn. It was both air and water tight, excepting a hole nearly in its center, just large enough to receive its occupant. It was eighteen feet long and twenty inches wide, running off to a sharp point at both ends.

The Esquimo sailor was nicely adjusted to the hole in the center. His undressed, hooded, seal-skin coat was drawn closely over a rim around the hole, fitting tightly, and completely shutting out the water. He seized in the middle an oar bladed at both ends, and, dipping it on either side rapidly and with wonderful skill, skimmed over the water as if boat and man were parts of the same animal —a thing of beauty, grace, and vivacity. As we rowed to the shore a fleet of these kayaks hung in our wake, or hovered about our sides, just outside the dip of our oars, like hungry sea-fowls after a morning breakfast. Our first impression of the people, who are Esquimo with some Danish blood, was one of disgust. Oil and fat, raw hides of seals, scraps of fish and discarded bones, and various kinds of garbage, were scattered every-where about the huts. Inside they were still more filthy—men, women, and children, old people and the invalids, were crowded into the smallest possible space. Their summer huts, in which some of them were now living, were made of reindeer skins. Their winter houses were half under ground. We saw in one, only six feet by eight, a father, mother, four children, and a grandfather, a tea-kettle, a rude box, two rifles, and a litter of puppies.

Floating Icebergs.

While we were rowing among the islands of Disco Bay we noticed the remarkable transparency of the water. This has often been noticed by voyagers to the Polar Seas as characteristic of them. We could see every feature of the bottom at a depth of sixty feet. A luxuriant growth of deep green plants, and long, tangled grasses, waved as gracefully as if they were the objects of constant observation by admiring men.

We obtained at Godhavn, on Disco Island, our outfit of fur clothes. The most important articles were a close-fitting jacket, called a "jumper," with a hood like that worn by our ladies on a water-proof, and water-tight seal-skin boots.

We were soon under all sail crowding our way toward the *north water*—the iceless sea beyond Melville Bay. Vessels sometimes cross from the Greenland to the west side of Baffin Bay, farther south, and occasionally they see an opening through the middle waters, but generally it is the quickest and safest route to keep on the east side until reaching the northern opening. On the first of July we began our conflict with field-ice—broken fragments of great extent.

July 2 we were sailing in water free from the drifting cakes of ice, but the huge, cold, dignified, but at times sparkling icebergs were about us. We observed one, a monster ice mountain, whose top and sides were varied in form, including hill and dale. It was at least two hundred feet high. On this a company of us landed. The scenery to which we were treated from one of its hill-tops was beautiful. Below, the water was surging into the caves and grottoes at its base, sending up a murmuring sound of plaintive music; above us were wild, projecting crags on which the sea-birds screamed their harsh but joyous notes of freedom.

We were treated, by that curious operator in arctic views, refraction, to a fine panorama as we were, on the 11th of July, slowly moving over an almost quiet sea. A strip of horizon, resembling an extended plain—a true watery horizon—first appeared. Then above it was a horizon of refraction, with an aerial ocean margin, lined with structures ever varying in form. Great needles, obelisks of pure whiteness, cities in majestic proportions, but instantly passing into the chaotic forms of the wildest ruins, and buildings of architectural grandeur, whose outlines we had just begun to scan, when the whole vanished. The excited imagination of the inebriate could not create a more fantastic scene. Suddenly, as by a flash, they re-appeared, to dance, dazzle, and amaze for a moment, and then to vanish as swiftly.

If the creations of refraction are the baseless fabrics of a vision, navigation in this ice-bound sea with our sturdy little vessels is a real thing. Let us try to show our readers how *we* did it.

We are now in a little space of clear water. Look beyond this over the bows of our vessel. It is one extended and almost boundless plain of solid ice. A little distance to the left is a huge iceberg rising above the icy plain like some hill from the level land of the shore. You see that narrow opening in this field of ice, commencing just on our left. Its irregular course may remind you of the wandering streams through the meadows at home, as it follows for awhile the base of the berg, and then is lost to the sight in its serpentine windings. This is known among arctic navigators as a "lead." We propose to break away from the icy prison in which we have been held for some time by navigating that "lead" by what is called "conning." The sails are put in trim and the brig's head is directed to the open gap. Men are stationed at the ropes which control the sails. Silence for a moment prevails as we wait for the concussion. The commander thunders his orders to the man at the helm, the sails, by a steady haul on the ropes, aid the vessel in the course the helm has given her, and she thrusts her nose into the gap. Away she goes banging her sides against the ice, crushing it with her bows, and making, it may be, a headway equal to a few times her length. Somebody in the rigging who is watching the "lead" exclaims "pshaw!" as we bring up, all-standing, in a short turn of the "lead." For a time we scrape, scratch, and thump our way, until two great, solid ice-fields shut us in, and forbid our moving another foot until their sovereign pleasure is further communicated. Some one exclaims, "eugh!" and we all go quietly to supper.

When we come on deck again we have been refreshed by food and rest. We all have a mind to work and are ready for the word of command. Our captain now changes the mode of attack on the enemy. The wind is light and dead ahead, and there is not enough sea-room to get headway on the ship if it were not, so smashing the ice by sailing into it is for the present "played out." The ice-anchors are ordered out. These are strong iron hooks, of which we have two sizes, one weighing forty and the other a hundred pounds. Two men jump from the ship with one of the largest and settle it into the ice ahead near the edge of the crack through which we wish to force our way. The large hooked end of the anchor being sunk firmly, to the smaller hook of its other end a new, strong, large rope—"a hawser"—is adjusted. The other end of the hawser is wound around "the windlass" with cogs and levers attached. All hands in turn man the levers, bringing a strain on the hawser which draws with immense power on the ice-anchor. Captain, cook, steward, doctor, and seamen sweat away at the levers, dignity stepping aside to let muscles have control. The crack gradually opens, the ship crowds herself in, until the hawser's length is drawn up to the anchor, which is then carried ahead and the operation repeated. This we call "heaving."

May be the ice refuses to be thus crowded aside; we toil and strain away with the powerful machinery which draws upon the ten-inch hawser; it smokes with the tension, snaps with a loud report, and we give it up and go below. We have had nothing to pay for our hard work but the satisfaction of those who *try*.

We wait, rest, recover our strength and energy, and try again. Now perhaps the Ice King is in better temper toward us. He relaxes his grip, we *heave along* until our way becomes so easy that the hundred pound ice-hook is taken aboard. A man now jumps out with the forty pound hook on his shoulder. The ice has changed its mode of attack; it has become treacherous, and gives way as he leaps over the cracks, and from one icy raft to another. Occasionally he gets a ducking. Attached to the anchor he carries is a light, thin, strong cordage, called a whale-line, made of the best material. He plants his anchor firmly in a distant ice-cape lying in the direction of our desired course. The ship end of the line is passed round "the capstan." The drawing in of this line is light work compared to the "heaving;" strong bars are put in the sockets made for them in the machine we call "a capstan," by which it is made to turn and thus wind round it and draw in the cord. All hands grasp these capstan-bars and walk round; if the sailors are fresh and in good humor, we march to the jolly chorus of their song. The ship "walks" through the broken ice until all the cord is drawn in and she reaches the anchor. The merry work is then repeated, and we make a little progress. This we call *warping*.

Soon our fickle Ice King gives us an opportunity for another style of progress. As the floes are ever changing, so we change our expedients. A canal of clear water is allowed us. Both heaving and warping are abandoned as too hard or slow work. The line is run out, and the men harness themselves to it. This is done by putting a strap over their shoulders and then fastening it to the line. Thus "accoutered," the men-horses tug away, or start off, if there is clear sailing and good footing, at "a dog trot," drawing the vessel after them. This we call *tracking*.

When we could neither "heave," nor "warp," nor "track," we wasted our strength on "sawing," "cutting," "prying," and other expedients, impelled by our want of experience and our ardent temperaments. We spent twenty-one days in this kind of toil, in a circle not more than twelve miles in diameter. We measured progress from day to day by yards and feet, not by miles. This will do to illustrate our way of getting out of *tight* places.

On the eleventh of July the "Devil's Thumb," a so-called landmark of the nearest shore, was plainly visible in the clear atmosphere, though fifty miles off. We were still in the "pack."

"What do you make of that?" said the commander, addressing Dr. Kane, and directing his attention to an object between us and the shore. Dr. Kane took the glass De Haven had been using, and looked. "A mast, with gaff and mainsail partially clewed up," answered Dr. Kane decidedly. Both thought that one of the Danish schooners had anchored at the edge of the pack. A more powerful telescope was brought up from below and directed toward the schooner, but it was not there! It was a trick of refraction!

The next day we sighted a polar bear, the first which had crossed our track. He was less than a half mile off, trotting leisurely, not deigning to notice us. Probably he held in low esteem all ships and the savage intruders upon bear territory which they contained. We proved that his length was nine feet by measuring his tracks. His color, as compared with the white snow, seemed a delicate yellow; his nose blue-black; his broad, regularly arching haunches, resting upon ponderous legs, gave him the look of an elephant.

Of course we gave chase to the bear, with guns in hand and murderous intent. The ice being weak in places, our zeal was far greater than our discretion. We did not get a shot at him in all the chase of three hours. Though we did not return with the polar, we did return wetter if not wiser men, for several of us got repeated duckings. As to his polar majesty, he never once varied from his dignified, unconcerned walk. When we last saw him he was in the dim distance among hummocks of ice.

A few days after this incident, as we were *waiting*, our men organized foot-races with the crew of the "Rescue." We had fancy matches against time. Our best runner made his mile in seven minutes and eleven seconds.

While our commander was punching the ice, as

he stood upon a projecting point of the floe, it gave way and soused him in. He had some difficulty in getting out. The incident was serious in its liabilities, but as "all is well which ends well," especially with men in our line of business, we laughed at it when safe in the cabin.

CHAPTER XXI.

FREAKS OF ATMOSPHERIC REFRACTION.

SOON after our first experience in bear-hunting, a shout came down the cabin where we were sitting, "A bear alongside!" It proved to be a young bear, not more than two-thirds grown. He came quite near, and leisurely surveyed the brig as he raised himself upon his haunches and snuffed the air, as if querying what manner of animals we might be. We kept below the bulwarks watching his innocent gambols, and, we are almost ashamed to say, seeking to reward his confidence with a bullet, He rubbed his nose against a hummock, snapped at the icicles, and rolled over and over. He was well within the range of our guns at one time, but just as we were about to fire he gamboled away, full of the enjoyment of life. We felt glad we had not fired, but, of course, we chased him, bent on taking his skin, not doubting our right to it—if we could get it. But the little rascal seemed to think that it belonged to himself, and he kept it uninjured.

On the 28th of July we were in that famous water, Melville Bay, in which the whalers as well as explorers have always had a dreary voyaging. A thrilling incident gave us an emphatic hint of what we might expect. We were among the floes, but had entered a narrow channel of clear water, which appeared to be a mile long. The wind was ahead, and we were engaged in our now well-tried business of warping; but huge bergs, driven by the strong northern deep-sea current, were sailing in the very teeth of the breeze. One of them kept us company for some time, and, while we were enjoying the clear water of "the lead," pushed forward to get ahead of us, and thus shut us out of any further advantage of it. This exciting race was going on, we having the "Rescue" in tow, when we reached a point where, by warping round our opponent, we might be able to make sail and get rid of him. Three men were sent to plant the ice-anchor in his side to hold the warp. The hole for it had been cut by the iron crow; a brawny seaman by the name of Costa was in the act of lifting the anchor, to settle it into the solid ice, when, with a thundering noise, a crack ran along the berg. Instantly a mass twice the size of our ship separated from it. One man remained on the rolling berg, another jumped into the ropes of our bowsprit and escaped; but poor Costa, anchor and all, disappeared in the chasm with the separated mass. But the broken fragment had made a perpendicular descent into the sea, and when it rose it brought Costa up with it! He was seized by the captain as he was passing the jib-boom and taken safely on board. God's hand was apparent in his rescue. Costa was terribly scared, and we were most emphatically warned to beware how we attempted to put our iron into the heart of an iceberg.

Five days after this incident we recognized one of these bergs which were now racing with us, a hundred miles on its northern voyage, still sailing against wind and surface ice.

On the morning of the first of August our friends had a successful encounter with a bear. He was walking toward the brig, cautiously treading over weak ice. Having probably found it too rotten to bear his heavy feet, he made a succession of plunges, coming each time nearer the vessel, breaking the ice as he rose. He stared about as his head came through the ice, as if amazed, and he panted and shook the water from his shaggy coat like a Newfoundland dog. He seemed to have an intense curiosity, and his attempt to gratify it in coming near the strangers cost him his life. Several well-directed bullets struck him and he turned away, weak and bleeding. With much difficulty he regained the floe, but it was only to meet a bayonet thrust which killed him.

Three days later three bears were seen on the ice which lay between us and the land. We were in a lead about three hundred yards wide, and while we were getting ready the boats to give them chase, they plunged into the water and came directly toward us. In two or three minutes they were within shot of the boat, coming on with their mouths open and showing their teeth, panting as if eager for the fight. The captain was the first to try his skill as a marksman, but his gun missed fire. The second officer, Midshipman Lovell, brought his gun up, lodged a ball in the base of the brain of one of the animals, and killed him instantly. Dr. Kane reserved his fire for a better chance, which did not come. While we were securing the dead bear the rest turned back, scrambled up the floe, and ran away.

Just as we reached the deck of the "Advance" with our prize, the heavy floe upon the seaward side of us began to move in toward the shore ice. The two vessels were in the clear water between them. The projecting edge of the outside floe came in contact with the inward or shore ice, about midway between the "Advance" and "Rescue." The assailing floe was nearly four feet thick and a mile in diameter. On the enormous mass came, with its millions of tons weight, striking the solid margin of the land ice with a force which seemed sufficient to grind both to powder. But the land ice endured the concussion without flinching, while its assailant was first pressed together, then crowded up in great inclined planes, which rose until broken and toppled over in long lines of fragments. The immense cakes of ice, as they rose, seemed thrust into the air by an almost silent, mighty, and invisible machinery.

There was a terrific sublimity in all this when seen at a safe distance. But when the attacking line neared our brig, bringing us between it and the unyielding land ice, the sublime was lost in the appalling. We expected her sides to be ripped, and, perhaps, crushed in, or the whole craft to be borne down by the pressure. After a moment's painful suspense the crisis came. The floes came together, not in a straight line along the whole length of our vessel at once, but made an acute angle at her bows, out of which she slipped like a squeezed watermelon seed shot from your thumb and finger. Her hawser snapped like pack-thread, and away she shot backward into more sea room.

The "Rescue" was tipped over so as almost to lay her masts on a line with the floe, and then placed on her keel again and lifted upon the ice. The rudders of both vessels were lifted from their places.

The second day after this encounter with the "nip" the wind changed, the surface-current started the seaward ice off, the lead opened, and we sought a safer berth.

A few days after the floes had entertained us by "nipping," refraction, our ever-welcome friend stepped forward with *his* entertainment. He was never more himself nor in a better condition to show his wonderful dramatic power. See there, just north of the sun; a black ball floating in the air! it is launched from his hand. What can it be? Perhaps a bird or a balloon. There! its circumference shines, glistens, and changes its shape! Now we know just what it is; plainly it is a grand piano! No, not quite so fast with your opinion; it is an anvil! Right this time! It is an anvil big enough for the giants of the north, if there be any, to hammer out upon it the North Pole, or any other poles they may fancy. Poh! it is no longer an anvil. It is narrowing in the center, and rounding off at the ends. It is a pair of huge dumb-bells, with which the giant gymnasts strengthen their brawny arms for a turn at boxing! There, it has changed again! It is nothing but the black ball now.

Our performer now becomes more sober, but not less skillful. He operates on a magnificent scale; he has taken the whole horizon. He blends the pearly sky and pearly water so that you cannot discern the line of separation! Our ship is in the hollow of a great sphere. Icy shapes of wonderful beauty and variety are floating all about us. Birds are seen flying both above and below. Our consort, the "Rescue," rests, in duplicate, serenely in the sky!

On the next night, at ten o'clock, our performer again exhibited. The sun was nearly at its lower curve. Suddenly there are signs of combustion flaring all around him. Great volumes of black smoke arise, contracting and expanding in its upward course, and as it rolls off into space black specks rise with it, expand, fall, and disappear! The rarified air above the whole waves and quivers with the heat. It is some mighty city in conflagration; some burning Chicago or Boston! No; it is only the jugglery of refraction!

We were now, August 15, near Cape York, the northern boundary of Melville Bay. The "Rescue." had lagged astern, though we were in clear water. While we were leisurely looking around from our deck she gave us the signal of "men in sight." A boat was immediately laden with provisions and sent to the shore, for, as we were so far north, the idea of human beings involuntarily connected itself with disaster. But two men were soon seen on the shore ice, gesticulating in the most ludicrous and violent manner. They were genuine specimens of the Esquimo. Though living in this icy, bitter cold, and desolate region, they were as fat as the bears we had lately killed. They were jolly, laughing fellows, full of sociability. They were armed with a harpoon, lance, and air-bladder, and had been hunting seals. They had no kayak, and seemed unacquainted with that convenient article of their more southern relatives. They intimated that there were more of their people in a valley toward which they pointed. They had evidently seen ships before, and invited themselves aboard; but the officer of the boat declined the invitation. They belonged, we concluded, to the wandering fishing and seal-catching Esquimo of this region whom John Ross, and, after him, the English navigators term "Arctic Highlanders."

A touching incident occurred near this place in 1830. The seamen of a whaler landed from their boat and walked to a group of huts. They observed as they approached, the death-like stillness which pervaded the vicinity and the absence of recent tracks in the snow. They lifted the skin of the door-way and entered. There, around an oilless lamp, were the corpses of five human beings. The frosty finger of death had left them, save the sunken eyes and darkened lips, in the attitude and with the expression of life. The babe was frozen in the hood of the reindeer coat which enveloped its mother, and the dog was stark and stiff at the feet of its master.

Several other huts exhibited the same melancholy sights. As the implements for seal catching lay in the tents, and as that animal abounds in the bays, and affords both food and fuel for these people, they must have been smitten by a prevalent disease, or their supplies shut off by some extraordinary occurrence.

A company from the "Advance" landed in a little cove near Cape York. Here we had an opportunity of examining the "red snow" which we had seen on the cliffs during our last ten miles' sail. Its color was a deep but not bright red. A kind of brick-dust lay upon its surface, and other portions of its coloring matter was evidently of a vegetable origin. It imparted to paper when drawn over it a cherry-red which faded into a brown. The snow resembled, with the impurities it contained, crushed preserved cranberries, and a handful thawed in a glass tumbler looked like muddy claret wine.

There was near a beautiful little cove. On one side of it was a glacier which came down from its valley birthplace above. One side of the glacier clung to the cliff, the other side which it presented to us was a solid, almost perpendicular, crystal wall; its end descended into the sea. A stream from the valley, which had worn a channel in the glacier, leaped, when it reached the edge of the glacier wall, into the sea below in a cascade of foam-sparkling water.

The side of the cove opposite to the glacier was watered by misty spray from the cascade, and was green with beautiful arctic mosses. It seemed a fairy spot in comparison to the barren sight of weeks past, and was indeed a charming spot which we could not forget. Dr. Kane named it "Bessie's Cove."

The next day, while sailing leisurely along, we saw an indentation in the high, precipitous, rocky shore. Into this we warped our vessel, so near that we stepped out on the rocks as upon a wharf. The sun was at its lowest curve, for it was the midnight hour of four P.M. The cove at the base of its walls was in black shadows, but far above it was bathed in a sparkling sunlight. A torrent of water rushed down the sides, with which we filled our tanks for the trip across the North Water into which we had now come.

The slope into the cove at one place was covered with terraces of rocky and icy fragments. Birds in myriads hovered about it, or settled down into its crevices. A party of our men were blazing away at them and bagging hundreds. Their nests were not all forsaken of their young, and fledglings were peering down upon us by thousands and opening their mouths for the food their mothers were bringing them from the sea.

Drawn by a wish to study the domestic habits of these arctic birds, Dr. Kane clambered up to one of their most populous colonies, without duly considering how he might get down. As he ascended the sharply inclined plane, with a walking pole substituted for his gun, the fragments receded from under his feet, and rushed down with a thundering noise to the plain below. He stopped to take breath, and was startled to see every thing about him in motion. The entire surface seemed to be sliding down. The position was one of real danger. The masses, gathering swiftness as they descended, leaped over the terraces, and filled the air with fearful missiles. Some whizzed by his face, and others shot over his head, and his walking-pole was jerked from his hand and buried in the rubbish. He commenced returning, fearing that the downward trip might be swifter than was pleasant or safe. Seeing a projecting rock not far from him, against which the sliding rubbish divided into two streams, he made a desperate jump and landed upon it. He here waited for the troubled fragments to adjust themselves. The scene around him was wonderfully original and arctic. The sun was "setting into sunrise" near the horizon, and the whole atmosphere "was pink with light." Auks and ivory gulls screeched with deafening clamor around him, sometimes flapping their wings almost in his face; dignified "burgomasters" sat unmoved on the crags above, seeming to enjoy the embarrassment of the obtrusive stranger; while far below, their black forms contrasting with the white snow, two ravens contended for a choice bit of garbage.

Quiet being restored, the doctor descended safely, wiser concerning arctic hill-sides if not in the habits of arctic birds.

On the 18th of August we turned the bows of our ships west, with the waves dancing past us and the breeze in our sails. We had accomplished the western passage, and were spanking along toward Lancaster Sound. The next morning about eight o'clock the pleasant news was brought to the cabin from the deck that two vessels were following in our wake. We slackened sail and so did the "Rescue," and hove to near us. Soon the larger of the two vessels was along side, and her captain came on board. It was Penny with his squadron—the "Lady Franklin" and the "Sophia"—bound with us to search for the lost. Such a greeting was exchanged as those only can give who are bound together by like toils and aims. When the "Franklin" started off, again there came booming over the sea a hearty old English hurra—"three cheers, hearty, with a will." Our boys "stood aloft," and gave back the greeting with vociferous earnestness.

At eight o'clock the same day we were in Lancaster Sound, groping our way through the fog, and staggering under a heavy sea and a tempest of wind. A day later, early in the morning, a vessel was reported ahead, tugging after her a small sailing craft. We shook out our reefs and scud before the gale, the sea dashing over us at every roll. We soon came up with the stranger. It was the "Felix," Sir John Ross commander, with her little tender, the "Mary." The hailing officer, in the midst of our talk, shouted, "You and I are ahead of them all!" So it was. Penny was astern, and Captain Austin, with his sailing ships and steam propellers, was hovering about the mouth of the sound.

Soon Sir John himself came on deck, and stood beside his hailing officer. He was a square-built man, apparently, but a little stricken in years, and well able, as he was willing, to bear his part of the rough toil of arctic search. He was in the very region where, seventeen years before, he was picked up, after four successive winters spent in polar snows.

The next morning we had passed the opening into Regent Inlet, and sighted Port Leopold, on its north-western side. We were anxiously looking for a "lead" into the harbor, for the ice beset it, when we saw a top-sail schooner working out to meet us. Her commander was soon on our deck. It was Lady Franklin's own searching vessel, the "Prince Albert!"

The "Rescue" had gone to Cape Riley, at the eastern side of the entrance to Wellington Channel, and we pushed forward immediately to that point in company with the "Prince Albert." On arriving there we learned that Lieutenant Griffin, of the "Rescue," had shared with the English steam-propeller squadron in the discovery of the evidence of Sir John Franklin's first winter encampment. The commanders, Ross, Penny, and De Haven, soon met on board the "Felix" to arrange plans of further search, and the greatest harmony of feeling prevailed. Our part was to push up Wellington Channel. While these officers were in council an excited messenger came running over the ice with thrilling news. "Graves!" he shouted. "Graves, sir! graves of Franklin's men!" We all hurried off to see for ourselves.

An account of these marks of Franklin's winter-quarters has been given by Lieutenant Osborne, of the propeller squadron, and we need not repeat them. The hint they gave us inspired our zeal to obtain further knowledge of his fate. At two o'clock in the morning of September 4 we were awakened by Captain De Haven to witness the rare appearance and movements of the ice. We had seen the wonders of the floes, but this was the most wonderful. The thickness of some of the cakes of ice which had been raised upon the floes by their collision was fourteen feet! They were piled in hummocks not seldom forty feet high! We were fast to a great floe by three anchors. The wind was blowing a fresh breeze from the north, and huge ice rafts, with up-piled blocks, far above our heads, were scudding past us to the west, under the propelling power of the current. They created a decided sensation among us as we stood watching them from our deck. There comes a monster thirty feet high! Will he smash in our stern? No, he shies off so near that we are fanned by the wind of his crystal sails. There comes another whose projecting crags will certainly become entangled in our rigging and sweep away our masts. No, he too just touches us with his frosty fingers, as if forbidden to do more, and then swings off into the deeper current.

A little projection of the main floe into the channel turns them aside as they approach us. How plainly do we see in this arrangement the care over us of Him who made the sea, and directs all that is in it.

While we were coasting during the day along the floe and sighting the western shore of Wellington Channel a bear attracted our attention. As exciting as such a sight always is, we could not stop to chase him. But he was very obliging. Instead of striking landward, he plunged into the water just ahead of us. Dr. Kane and one other of the officers brought their guns to bear at a fair range and fired at the same moment. *One* of the bullets went amiss, indicating its course by splashing in the water just ahead of its mark. The other killed the bear outright. The boats were got out, and he was brought alongside and with difficulty hoisted aboard. He was a monster, weighing, we estimated, sixteen hundred pounds. He measured nine feet from tip to tip, and his carcass was larger than that of an ordinary ox when fatted for the market. His build was solid, and the muscles of his arms and haunches fearfully developed.

The question was pleasantly raised, Whose bullet hit? It was found that the one which had done the murderous deed had entered the ear and lodged in the brain. This was weighed and proved to belong to Dr. Kane's gun. It was his first bear! He skinned him on deck the next morning with the thermometer below zero. This skin is now in the rooms of the Academy of Natural Science at Philadelphia.

Our game was at this time two bears, three seals, a single goose, and a fair table allowance of smaller sea-fowl. The goose was killed by officer Murdaugh, on the wing, with a rifle. The "Rescue" boasts of four bears, two hares, and a supply of smaller game. It must be recollected that our hunting was not systematically done, but was only incidental to our other absorbing business.

On the eleventh of September all the searching vessels except Penny's were clinging by their anchors to the fast ice near Griffith Island. The next day we had a fearful experience. The wind blew a gale, driving before it clouds of heavy snow. The "Rescue" snapped her hawsers and disappeared to the seaward, leaving two men, her boat, and her ice-anchors behind. The "Advance" snapped her stern cable, lost her anchor and swung out, but she fortunately held by the forward line. The English squadron parted some of their hawsers, and were in momentary danger of coming down upon us. The wind roared, and poured upon us its sleet and snow, and every thing about the vessel froze. To add to the terribleness of our situation, the main floe threatened to part, and carry us away with the liberated ice, with our running rigging so ice-encumbered as to make the working of the vessel impossible. We are at sea, some distance from the shore, whose harbors are unknown to us, even if the wind and ice permitted us to seek one. We see signs of cheerful fires on board the English vessels. We yet have none. About noon the whole fleet, having knocked off the ice as best it could, got under way for Griffith Island, from which we had drifted about fifteen miles. We were in anxious search for our lost consort. We were staggering under all sail, running for our lives, striking the ice with our seven and a half solid feet bows, with such fearful blows that our vessel quivered like a leaf. While thus struggling, we came in sight of the "Rescue" close under the island. We at once drove our hard-headed little brig into the intervening ice, determined to lay alongside of her. She nobly thumped her way through, the English following "the mad Yankees."

No sooner had we thus opened a channel to the "Rescue" than orders were given by Captain De Haven to both vessels to bear away for home! All regretted this, but so the home authorities had commanded. We were not to spend the winter in the ice unless under *very* extraordinary circumstances such as were not now upon us. We parted with our fellow-explorers with sincere regret. Only courtesies and hearty good-will had been received from them, and many lasting friendships had been formed. Some of our officers proposed exchanging places with any of theirs who might desire to return home; but none such were found. Our captain tendered them a part of our supply of provisions, and a point on the shore was agreed upon on which, if we were able to land, we were to make a deposit.

In a short time we had the "Rescue" in tow steering westward.

As we were passing a curve of the coast soon after, the captain called Dr. Kane's attention to the shore-line six miles off. He looked, and saw the naked spars of two vessels. "Brigs," says Kane. "Without doubt," replies De Haven. Both at once exclaimed, "Penny!" On taking a glass, the masts, yards, gaffs, every thing but the bowsprit, were distinctly seen. Officer Lovell was called and saw the same. Murdaugh hurries up, half dressed, from the cabin, takes a good spyglass and looks. He sees a third vessel. The rest look, all see the third one and pronounce it the "Felix"—old Sir John Ross.

We change our course, and run in to speak with them. A fog settles down between us, but still we keep on. The fog in a few moments clears away, there is only three miles between us and them. We look, there is not a vessel to be seen! We take a powerful glass, and see only some hummocks of ice! We were "sold" again by that polar cheat, refraction. We were reluctant to accept the joke, and went musing and murmuring away, saying: "How *could* we be so deceived!"

Soon after this the captain shouted down the cabin stairs: "Doctor, we are frozen up!" Yes, we were frozen up in mid-channel, at the mouth of the great Wellington Channel! What now about our going home! how about not wintering in the ice!!

CHAPTER XXII.

DE HAVEN'S WONDERFUL DRIFT.

THE ice-island which had thrown its frosty arms around our ships as we were attempting to pass the entrance of Wellington Channel held them firmly. Up the channel northward it hurried with us. In vain we entreated and protested that we desired to go *east*, not north! Our island was fiercely assailed at times by heavy floes, now making their attacks on this side, then on that, and occasionally on both sides at once. At one time the ice near our ship, pressed by a fearful power, cracked; its outer edge of fourteen inches of solid ice turned up and rose in great tables, high in the air, until by its weight it toppled over. This was followed by other tables, sliding up the broken fragments of the last, so forming heavy piles of ice rubbish, which after a while would sink into the sea.

While thus the floes were toying with us, and at times seeming intent on crushing us, the current would occasionally swing us round through all the points of the compass, giving us quite a sail south, as if to flatter us with the hope of the homeward voyage, while yet we were making daily advance northward.

The collision of the floes at this time gave us

our first sight of a phenomenon of which other explorers have spoken. When in the darkness of the night the great ice-tables were hurled upon each other, a phosphorescent light was emitted, like that of fire-flies, or the "fox fire" of southern meadows. It was very beautiful.

At the end of our first week of drifting we had made sixty miles from the entrance of the channel, and still we headed northward.

One day a black fox came near our vessel, nimbly skipping from hummock to hummock. He looked cheerful, but desolate, away, as he was, seven miles from the nearest land—a land looking as dreary as the ice-fields themselves. Our sailors set a trap for him. In the night we heard his bark, and were sure he would be their prize in the morning. But Dr. Kane, having killed a seal the day before, and pitying the little wanderer, had crept slyly out and put some of the offal, quite a pile, outside of the snare. Fox had a splendid supper without pay or penalty, and went on his way rejoicing.

We try to be merry as we drift away into the unknown north. The "Rescue" was all the while fixed in the ice near us. We began to think of the necessity of wintering thus bound in arctic fetters. The ice about our ships was adjusted to our convenience. We began to put some tons of the coal from our hold. The boats were drawn about twenty paces from the bow, and all hands were at work getting ready the deck to be covered in by "a felt" we had brought for the purpose.

Two officers had been sent to the shore to select a place for a provision depot. But, whew! what a noise the floes suddenly made, as if indignant that *their* permission had not been asked before entering upon the arrangements. Their mustering forces hummed like bees and whined like puppies, while now and then came crashes like an avalanche and explosions like thunder. The land party hurried back in breathless haste. All hands rushed for the boats and stores we had transferred to the floe. Before dark all was on board except about two tons of coal, and the ice was in motion in every direction. Our little cabin had been cheerless enough. Every thing dripped with steam, and was damp and cold. "A Cornelius Lard Lamp" had been hung up and put in operation in the middle of September, and afforded great relief. Our stove was not up until the 19th. Now, October 2, we were surrounded by an arctic frost-smoke, which made the darkness without murky, waving—a peculiar, unnatural darkness. The light and heat within, though poor, were strangely welcome.

The ice soon knit together again, the frost-smoke lifted up, and its *felt* darkness disappeared. Dr. Kane went out, gun in hand, and sat down, Esquimo-like, by a seal-hole. With the thermometer 10° below zero, and the necessity of *perfect* stillness to assure success, it was no fun. One tedious hour he waited; some young seals appeared, he fired, missed, and they darted away. Another hour and they came again. He says: "Very strange are these seals! A countenance between the dog and wild African ape—an expression so like that of humanity that it makes gun-murderers hesitate. At last, at long shot, I hit one. God forgive me! The ball did not kill outright. It was out of range, struck too low, and entered the lungs. The poor beast had risen breast high out of water, like the treading-water swimmers among ourselves. He was thus supported, looking about with curious, expectant eyes, when the ball struck his lungs.

"For a moment he oozed a little bright blood from his mouth, and looked toward me with a sort of startled reproachfulness. Then he dipped; an instant after he came up still nearer, looked again, bled again, and went down. A half instant after he came up flurriedly, looked about with anguish in his eyes, for he was quite near me; but slowly he sunk, struggling feebly, rose again, sunk again, struggled a very little more. The thing was drowning in the element of his sportive revels. He did drown finally, and sunk; so I lost him.

"Have naturalists ever noticed the expression on this animal's phiz? Curiosity, contentment, pain, reproach, despair, even resignation, I thought I saw on this seal's face.

"About half an hour afterward I killed another. Scurvy and sea-life craving for flesh meat led me to it; but I shot him dead!"

A fox was caught about the same time. We ate of fox and seal and pronounced them good.

Sunday, October 6, was a dismal day. We

were fast in a huge cake of ice, driving southward before a furious gale. Away we sped, onward, onward for two days, during which we made sixty miles, reached the outlet of Wellington Channel, from which we had been violently dragged.

While thus beating about we caught a white fox alive. He resented the chains of spun-yarn and leather which bound him, but always had composure enough for picking the meat from the bones which were thrown to him and for eating snow; he would not touch water. His cry resembled that of a small boy undergoing a spanking; its tones expressed not only fear and pain, but spite and ill-temper. He soon, however, became good-natured. He would eat from our hands the next day. Twice he was set at liberty, but he returned both times to our trap a few hours after his liberation.

These white foxes seemed to have no instinctive fear of man. They approached the ship's side with more curiosity than fear. If we fired deadly shot among them they scampered off but for a moment and returned. When we went out to them on the ice we were allowed almost to touch them with our hands. If we shouted they ran round us in a narrow circle, stopped and stared when we were still. One little fellow was caught, put in a box on deck, fed for a few days, and liberated. He scampered away a few rods, stopped, considered, and returned to his cubby on deck.

Being for three weeks detained at the fickle will of our ice-raft about Wellington Strait, Dr.

Kane put into effect his long-meditated attempt to communicate with the English fleet at Union Bay, where we had left them. After facing appalling dangers, and making repeated trials, the enterprise was reluctantly abandoned.

It was now the eighth of November, and our winter-quarters, such as they were, were completed. The deck had its covering of felt drawn down to the sides of the vessel. The room occupied by the seamen and that of the officers was made one by knocking away the cabin partition, the two stoves thus warming all alike. The officers and men of the "Rescue" had been ordered on board the "Advance," and we made one family. We banked up the sides of the vessel with snow, up to the felt, thus increasing our defense against the cold. Thus prepared, we could only wait the will of our crystal raft.

To occupy the minds of the men profitably during the slowly-moving days, Dr. Kane gave a series of popular lectures on science. They were well received.

During the latter part of November our iceland had enlarged its dimensions to a floe of several square miles, and this great raft had swung round, putting its sharp end toward the south, and giving indications of conducting us on our homeward voyage. But we commenced December cradled again on a paltry little island, the "Rescue" still near us. Away we drifted, the sport of contending floes which threatened hourly to sink or crush us. At times our island was not more than three hundred yards in diameter, yet it held us in its grip. The floes would batter and crack it, let our vessels down, lift them up, change their position, but always closing them up again and insuring their imprisonment. Our liability of being witnesses of the sinking or crushing of the vessels was so imminent that we lived in a studied preparation to abandon them. Mr. Griffin, commander of the "Rescue," was appointed as the executive officer to organize and drill the united crews in reference to such an emergency. He mustered them upon the ice with knapsacks fitted to their backs, filled with such indispensable articles as they would carry, and every man harnessed to his appointed sledge in due order. Provisions are all packed, and stores of all kinds put in compact order and duly marked. The men are taught every one his place, and specific duty, at the instant of the crisis. The little home Bibles and precious mementos were slyly tucked in the knapsacks.

The coolness of the men under these circumstances is well illustrated by the following incident: The "Advance" had been lifted upon the ice and so far laid upon her side that orders were given to abandon her, as it was likely she would be thrown upon her beam ends. As we stood upon the ice, thinking all were out, Boatswain Brooks shouted, "Stand from under," as the craft vibrated with the pressure upon her. Just then an officer, recollecting that the fires in the stoves had not been put out, and that they would set the vessel on fire, and thus insure the loss of every thing, climbed back into the hold. There at the mess-table sat an officer who had been a few moments before relieved from watch-duty quietly eating his dinner, and the cook as quietly waiting upon him. "You see," remarked the hungry man, "you are one meal ahead of me. You didn't think I was going out upon the ice without my dinner?" Captain De Haven, in his official report, mentions the gallantry and unflinching bravery of all the officers, and the good conduct and subordination of the men in this and all such perils.

But our vessel righted up a little, her bows sunk low in the ice, and her stern lifted up, making an inclined plane of the deck from the stern forward. Thus she was much raked by the wind greatly to our discomfort, as we felt the cold through her sides, now no longer banked with snow. In this truly arctic position we drifted steadily along the north shore of Lancaster Sound, and began already to anticipate our rush into the cross current of Baffin Bay.

To be further prepared for the impending crisis, some of us tried tramps on the ice-floe, and camping out, in tents and sleeping-bags. The experiment did not give cheering promise of any good time to come when the ships should be destroyed.

A poor bear ventured one night near the vessel. An officer fired at his retreating shadow. The next morning he was found dead some three hundred yards from the ship. He was wedged between two cakes of ice, and had in his agony rubbed his muzzle deep into the frozen snow. In his death-march he had twice stopped to lie down, marking each spot with pools of blood.

A poor little fox fell, too, before our sharpshooters. We pitied the beasts, struggling to live in this waste, howling, arctic wilderness, but they were eaten most joyously.

The effect of our isolated condition, and the ever present darkness, rendered more intense by a nightly, hazy obscurity, began to be apparent in our physical and moral condition. Our complexions were toned down to a peculiar waxy paleness. Sunken eyes, strangely clear, hollow cheeks and short breaths became general. Appetites changed, became capricious and slight. Many became moody, irritable, and imaginative. Dreams invested our sleep, and were fondly talked about when we were awake. Some, while in dreamland, had laden themselves with luscious water-melons with which to return on shipboard. Others had found Sir John Franklin in a beautiful cove, whose air was perfumed with blossoming orange trees. Our hard-fisted matter-of-fact boatswain heard three strange groans out upon the ice. He was sure of it, though he could see nothing. The scurvy had touched several lightly, and they were put under careful and stringent medical treatment.

Christmas came. We paraded our good things, of which we had some store. We joked, but did it badly; we laughed incessantly, but our laughing was bad, too; we sung, but our songs were boisterously noisy, with neither time, tune, nor harmony.

The dinner being a pretentious failure, the men tried a theater. It was on deck under our canopy. The acting *was* funny, and we laughed. None knew their parts. The prompters could not read glibly enough to be of any service. The gentle-women were brawny, blundering men, dressed in calico. The intervals of the orchestra were played on a Jew's-harp by a comic fellow from the top of a lard cask.

We had foot-races on the midnight ice.

Nor were the kindly Christmas gifts forgotten. Dr. Kane found in his stocking in the morning a jackknife, a Jew's-harp, a piece of Castile-soap, and a string of beads.

The effort exhibited in these performances to throw off the mental and moral, as well as physical distempers induced by darkness, cold, and dangers, was necessary, whether this was the best way to do it or not. The officers, with the superior resources of culture, needed them less than the men. In fact, in the cabin, in all these perilous, gloomy days, an honest courtesy toward one another was preserved, whatever of brooding home-thoughts and inward forebodings of evil were indulged.

With the men it was different. The wild voices of the ice and wind; the strange sounds which issued from the ship; the sudden terrific rupture in the darkness, and without apparent cause, of the hummocks; the cracks, and the dark-rushing water that filled them, and the wonder-working freaks of refraction, all stimulated, sickened, and oppressed their imagination—they were for the forecastle a day and nightmare dream full of horrors!

We are now near the new year of 1851. We are in sight of Cape Warrender, the great entering landmark of the northern shores of Lancaster Sound. We are only a few hours of favorable sailing from Baffin Bay, and only twenty-four from Greenland. We have averaged for ten days about five miles a day. We shall soon meet the cross current of the great bay as it strikes that which rushes out of the sound, and then will our situation be more critical perhaps than ever. Our trust is in God.

The new year, 1851, came in gloomily in spite of an extra dinner and efforts to be merry. By the middle of January we noticed the unmistakable evidence that we were in Baffin Bay. Our knapsacks, sledges, India-rubber boat, and general "traveling outfit," were in momentary readiness. We put the frozen bear meat and some barrels of bread on the floe for the emergency. But a sudden rupture of the ice swept them all away. So after that we kept in readiness our stock of provisions intended for the sledges on deck.

On the second of February the full disk of the sun appeared at a quarter before eleven. Although he rose but to set, yet the stream of light which heralded his coming and that which lingered after his departure, as well as his presence, cheered every heart, and sent new life through the ship. We knew he would tarry longer at each coming until he came to stay.

Sirius, no pale dog-star in these arctic regions, is resplendent in beauty. As it rises from its banked horizon the fun-loving refraction plays with it nightly freaks. Its colors are blue, crimson, and white. Now its shape is oval, now hour-glass, and then square. It goes out into blank darkness, and then flashes into life. It plays the revolving light, as if it would attract and then evade our notice. Beautiful, solacing, hope-inspiring Sirius! Welcome observer of our dreary voyage!

To-day, the 25th of February, Dr. Kane caught, in his reindeer hood, a bug! Its sole sign of life was a feeble wriggle. Nothing which shares our principle of vitality, save a seal and a fox, has greeted us for months. The hardy sea-fowls are far away. Even the raven, that dismal croaker, dark bird of even arctic winter, clings to the distant in-shore deserts. "The terns are gone, and so are the musquitoes! There are no bugs in the blankets, no nits in the hair, no maggots in the cheese! No specks of life glitter in the sunshine, no sounds of it float upon the air. We are without a single instinct of living thing!"

It was now early spring. We felt that our icy bonds must soon be loosened, and that we should want both ships in the best possible repair. The "Rescue" had been handled with especial severity; her stern-post was battered away, her bowsprit knocked off, and her bottom roughly beaten. Our men made out of her ice-bed a dry dock! They dug a pit about her within eighteen inches of the bottom of her keel, thus giving clear access to her bottom. In three days of hard and earnest work she was in good condition, ready for the word of command from her gallant captain.

From this time onward hope grew stronger with us, with the increasing length of the daylight and the increasing signs of spring. The birds came and greeted us with their harsh but welcome notes. Seals thrust their heads through the ice and played in the pools of water, often to their sorrow, as the fatal bullet pierced them, but to the joy of our scurvy-smitten men. The curious narwhals puffed and snorted in the water openings. Our old friend, the bear, whom we had so often loved, even unto his death, afforded us occasion for several exciting and perilous incidents.

On the 24th of April the officers and crew of the "Rescue" were ordered to their own ship. She had been put in good internal trim, and the fires had blazed in her stoves for several days.

June opened refreshingly. The air was warm, the breeze agreeable. The snow-birds in increasing numbers visited our deck, and delighted us with their sweet jargon. They are confiding little creatures, approaching our very feet.

Open water is in view from the top of a high hummock, and is rapidly coming nearer.

On the 5th the long-waited-for break up came. A grand swell of the sea under the ice caused it to rise and fall in great waves. The disruption came suddenly, and with terrific force. It shattered our ice-raft as window-glass was shattered by the careless balls of our boyhood. But a heavy fragment clung to our stern for three days, in which it was cradled, holding it several feet out of water, and keeping our deck in its old inclined plane. We thrust at it, drilled and sawed it, until at last it slipped away, and we were on an even keel! For five days from the disruption we fought our way slowly through heavy floating ice. On the 10th, with a great sea, a press of sail, and a spanking breeze, we bore away for Greenland. The next morning its shores were in sight.

How wonderful had been our escape from fatal accidents at the moment of breaking up. Dr. Kane had been in the habit of taking long and solitary walks upon the ice, miles from the ship. He had greased his boots for a walk a few hours before the change, and would have been off but for an absorbing interest in a book he was reading.

The commander of the "Rescue" was on board the "Advance" when the shock which unfettered us came. He rushed homeward, leaping the ice-cracks, which opened immediately behind him in impassable chasms, reached his deck safely, and waved us an adieu.

How wonderful, too, had been our drift! continuing through nearly nine months of time, and more than a thousand miles of distance! Yet we were safe, and, though scurvy-smitten, ready to renew the fight, along the western coast of Greenland—the old, perilous track—into the north water, through Lancaster Sound and Barrow Strait, up Wellington Channel, and thus renew and finish the search for Franklin! All this we attempted to do! We fought ice and cold again until August 19, reaching North Baffin Bay. Here, crippled, scurvy-ridden, and baffled at every turn, the game of another Wellington Channel search played out! We could honorably show the white feather and turn toward New York, where we arrived September 30, 1851, and were welcomed on the pier by our noble friend, Henry Grinnell.

CHAPTER XXIII.

THE NORTH-WEST PASSAGE DISCOVERED.

THE English fleet, whose career we have noticed, sailing under Austin, Sir John Ross, and Penny, returned home, as we have seen, the same fall in which De Haven reached New York. But other explorers were still in the arctic ice. Let us glance at their history.

The well-tried and splendidly equipped ships, "Enterprise" and "Investigator," were dispatched to Bering Strait, starting January 10, 1850. It was commanded by Captain Richard Collinson, in the "Enterprise," Captain Robert M'Clure commanding in the "Investigator." They were commissioned to find Sir John Franklin, and, by sailing from the Pacific easterly to the Atlantic, to prove the north-west passage. The ships were separated before reaching Bering Strait, and did not again meet. We shall give the story of M'Clure, as his voyage was one of deeply interesting results.

It will be recollected that no *ship* had sailed far into the ice from this point. But boat and sledge parties from various points had explored great distances along the coast. M'Clure met the "Plover" at the edge of the ice-field, which had been stationed there with supplies; he also fell in with the "Herald," which came annually to renew the provisions of the "Plover." From these he received three additional men and additions to his stores, and then plunged into the ice. He thus devoutly notes this fact in his journal: "I consider that we have said adieu to the world for the next two years. May that arm which has conducted us so far in safety still continue in protection upon a service where all else is weakness indeed!"

While fighting the ice they were entertained by herds of walruses, some of which weighed, they thought, thirty-five hundred pounds. The mothers were attended by their babies. The sportsmen immediately seized their guns to send the fatal bullets among them. But so tender did the mothers seem toward their great babes, and so playful and confiding were these offspring, that M'Clure waved his hand authoritatively, saying: "Don't fire, men! it's too bad!" and none were killed.

The next incident of interest was the meeting of three Esquimo by a boat's crew which had gone ashore. They were very timid, having never seen ships or white men before. M'Clure had taken a Moravian by the name of Mierching as an interpreter, who had been many years a missionary to the Esquimo of Labrador. He succeeded in allaying their fears, and when the parties had rubbed noses good feeling was established. The captain gave them letters to be delivered to any white men they might meet, containing dispatches to the home authorities. These letters reached their destination, though not until later information from the expedition had come to hand from another source.

Later they had Esquimo visitors in great numbers, who came off to the ships in their kayaks. When they had examined the ship and their curiosity was somewhat satisfied, they commenced an animated trade. They had salmon to sell, and were especially desirous to obtain tobacco. Seeing the sailors cut this article up before trading, a new thought seemed to be suggested to the natives, which run in this wise: These strangers cut up the tobacco to get much for a small piece. Why not cut our fish up! So at it they went, cutting up the salmon until prevented by the white men.

Stealing was an easy accomplishment of the Esquimo along this coast as well as elsewhere. While Captain M'Clure was putting a present into the right hand of a chief he felt his left robbing his pocket. On being exposed the chief laughed, and all his people laughed, esteeming it a good joke; and so much did they seem to enjoy it that the white men laughed too.

The farther the explorers sailed east the more shy and hostile the natives were. This was owing, it was thought, to the fights constantly going on between them and the wandering Indians who visited their coast, and begat in them a bad temper. But Mr. Mierching always succeeded in bringing them to the nose rubbing, after which matters went smoothly. In one case a brawny chief was immensely pleased with some gaudy gifts. Connecting his good luck with Mr. Miertching, he endeavored to bribe him to make his home among them. To succeed in this he brought forward a blooming young daughter, and offered her in marriage. He even promised to throw in, to enhance the bargain, a tent and "fixings." He was most crestfallen because his offer was refused.

By the usual sawing, smashing, dodging in and out of leads, going back and then forward, Captain M'Clure found, by observations taken on the ninth of September, that he was only sixty miles from a point in Barrow Strait to which several explorers had sailed from Lancaster Sound. He writes: "Can it be possible that this water communicates with Barrow Strait, and shall prove the long-sought north-west passage! Can it be that so humble a creature as I am will be permitted to perform what has baffled the talented and wise for hundreds of years! But all praise be ascribed unto Him who has conducted us so far in safety! His ways are not our ways, nor the means he uses within our comprehension. The wisdom of the world is foolishness with Him."

They were now in Prince of Wales Strait, and, on the sixteenth, were within thirty miles of open sea, through which they hoped to dash, and soon reach the familiar waters of Lancaster Sound, Baffin Bay, the Atlantic, and the English Channel, where, with "north-west passage accomplished" inscribed on their flag, wealth and fame awaited them! Please do, your Majesty of the Ice Scepter, grant us the small favor of a few weeks of clear sailing! But his majesty waved his scepter in grim defiance, closed the leads, chained the "Investigator" to an icy raft, and set her back twenty-four miles in three days! Here, after harassing anxiety, many nips, frequent threats of sinking and crushing, the "Investigator" was fast in the floe for winter.

On the twenty-sixth of October M'Clure made a sledge journey, with a party of his men, toward Melville Island. After much toil and the usual perils the water was discovered, from the top of a hill six hundred feet above the sea, which washed its shores. He had *seen* the north-west passage. From a point of land upon which he was looking, Parry, thirty years before, had sailed home through Baffin Bay.

In returning M'Clure came near perishing. Having seen some bearings ahead from which he felt confident he could make the ship, he started off ahead of his men, thinking to get ready for them a good supper on their arrival. When within six miles of the ship night shut in, at the same time a mist obscured every thing, which was followed by a fierce storm of blinding snow. He climbed upon a hummock of ice whose elevated flat top would give, he thought, a good position to see the lights of his men if they passed, or of the ship, if the mist cleared away. After waiting an hour he saw the glare through the mist of a blue light. He fired to attract attention. Waiting a little and perceiving no signs of approaching men, he fired his only remaining charge of powder. He listened, hoping the ship would answer, but no cheering response broke the gloom. Once more the blue light of the sledge party dimly flashed through the mist, now at a greater distance, and then his hope from them vanished. Two more hours passed; he then, in fumbling in his pocket found a single lucifer match. With this he endeavored to see the face of his pocket-compass, but it fizzed out and left him in total darkness. It was half-past eight o'clock and there were eleven more hours of darkness; the cold was 15° below zero, bears were prowling about, and he was without a charge for his gun. He hoped that the sledge party would reach the ship, and, finding he had not come in, search would be made and help arrive. He walked to and fro upon the hummock until he thought it was about eleven o'clock, and then that hope fled. Slipping down from his slab of ice he landed under its lee in a bed of soft, dry snow. Being thoroughly tired, he fell asleep and slept soundly. It was a sleep like that into which many under such circumstances have fallen, to be followed by the sleep of death. But M'Clure awoke refreshed, and opened his eyes upon a sky glittering with stars and illuminated with the aurora borealis. He could see no ship, and so he stumbled about among the hummocks for several more hours. When the daylight appeared he had the mortification to see that he passed near the ship in the night, and walked away from it nearly four miles.

Returning, he reached the "Investigator" weary and hungry, but not otherwise the worse for a night in the snow in 73° north latitude. The sledge arrived a few hours later all right.

While M'Clure was absent, his men left with the ship had been grandly successful in hunting. An attack on a herd of musk-oxen had brought down three bulls, a cow, and a calf. These gave twelve hundred and ninety-six pounds of solid meat. The land explorers down the Mackenzie, of an earlier date, esteemed musk-ox an offense to the stomach as well as the nose. But probably they were not so hungry for fresh meat as was M'Clure's men.

When the spring of 1851 came, wide ranges of country, both sea and land, were surveyed by sledge-parties. They gave occasion for many incidents of great peril and wonderful deliverance, which we cannot detail. While one party were hunting and camping in a tent, a hunter returned tired and chilled to within a rod or two of the tent door. Here he was found, every muscle rigid as he lay stretched upon the snow, his mouth open, and his eyes set in his head. But for the providential going out of one of the occupants of the tent, he would have been, in a short time, dead. Faithful and judicious treatment brought him to life. He said that though he remembers seeing the tent door, he was so irresistibly impelled to sleep that he lay down to indulge in a nap.

At another time a negro having wounded a

deer, followed it to a great distance. In returning he fell down exhausted and sleepy. No entreaties nor shakings of Sergeant Woon, who accompanied him, could excite the least ambition to get up and walk. Though the negro was a large, heavy man, Woon strapped his gun, with which he dare not part, to his back, took his arms over his shoulder and heroically started for the ships, many miles distance. At times he obtained relief by sliding his load ahead down the hummocks. He dare not leave him a moment as wolves were prowling around. When within a mile of the ship he became utterly exhausted, and unable to carry him another step. Laying down the poor fellow, he hastened to the vessel and obtained help. The man was safely borne to the care of the surgeon, under whose treatment he was in a few days all right.

This Sergeant Woon of the marines was a brave, self-possessed hunter. Being out on one occasion pursuing a wounded deer, he was suddenly confronted by two musk-bulls. Like all kine of their sex they were full of fight, but would have been content perhaps to be let alone. But Woon, though he had but one bullet, put it into one of them. Wounded and maddened, he turned upon his assailant. As he approached he received the "worm" from the sergeant's gun. This caused a pause, which he improved by reloading and using the iron ramrod for a missile. The bull by this time was within a few feet of his foe, with his nose to the ground, out of which poured a stream of blood, to return in *his* way the sergeant's complimentary salutations. But the ramrod was too quick and too much for him. It entered behind his left shoulder, passed through his heart, and came out at the right flank.

The sergeant returned to the ship and reported venison and beef in temporary storage upon the ice for the ship's use.

It was late in the summer of 1851 before the "Investigator's" ice-fetters were loosened, and then, instead of sailing north, she was treated to an ice-bound drift twenty-five miles south. Giving up the hope of getting to Melville Island through the channel in which they had wintered, M'Clure sailed south, around Bank Land, up its western side, and, by hard fighting and nipping, sailed round its northern extremity into Melville Strait, thus actually reaching the water which made the navigable highway home by the eastern route. The open water of this highway was within the range of a moderate sledge-journey. Of all arctic tantalizing that which this expedition now suffered seemed to be the most exquisite. The prize was lying at their feet—a prize sought for more than two hundred years but not found—while their hands were pinioned behind them!

M'Clure, seeing his vessel immovably frozen in, prepared for winter, and, thankful to be alive, called the bay in which they were detained the Bay of Mercy.

The expedition was put upon short rations, in view of a probable stay in the ice a third winter.

But game abounded, musk-ox, deer, foxes, and wolves being plenty. The wolves in the long dark nights, impelled by hunger, came around the ship and made the hideous night more hideous by their howlings. Ravens audaciously made the family of the strangers their home. They croaked in the rigging, and came under the covering of the upper deck. One shrewd fellow tricked a dog out of his meal. He lighted on deck behind him, and, of course, canine left his bone to drive him away. Raven hopped back a few yards at a time and thus enticed the dog some distance away, when he flew back, and gobbled down his dinner before he could return. This became a staple trick of the ravens until the dogs began to "see through it."

So bold did the wolves become that the men told the story of the sportsmen pulling at one end of the slain deer and the wolves at the other!

In April, 1852, M'Clure made a sledge-journey to Winter Harbor, on Melville Island, the winter-quarters of Parry in his famous voyage when this region was first made known to the world. M'Clure here found a cairn, under which Lieutenant M'Clintock had deposited a notice of his visit the previous summer when on a sledge-journey from Austin's steam squadron, which we have noticed. M'Clure left under the same cairn an account of his visit and present whereabouts.

On returning to the ship they were glad to learn that large additions had been made by the hunters to their stock of provisions. But the spring and summer brought no relaxing of the grip of the Ice King. A third winter in the Bay of Mercy became a sure experience, and the final abandonment of the "Investigator" quite probable. Under these circumstances M'Clure assembled his men and made known his plans. They were these: Two parties were to go home in the spring; one by the way of the Mackenzie River, another by the way of Beechey Island, where, as the record left by M'Clintock on Melville Island assured them, provisions and a boat to take them to the Danish settlements of Greenland would be found. As for M'Clure himself he proposed to stay by the ship, with thirty of the strongest men, and remain a fourth winter. He would then retreat on Lancaster Sound if help did not come sooner. All cheerfully agreed to these proposals.

Spring came, and the preparations to carry forward this scheme of escape were matured, and the two parties were about to start.

How fearfully perilous the route would prove to the mouth of the Mackenzie, up its portages, through its deep snow, around its impenetrable swamps, and over its many, many miles, before reaching the nearest station of the Hudson Bay Company, the reader, recollecting John Franklin's and Back's journeys, well understands. The party going east would face the enemies De Haven had just encountered. M'Clure's fourth winter and final escape involved great risk and suffering. The three parties would be poorly equipped and provisioned

The commencement of this movement was delayed on account of the death of a seaman, the first which had occurred in the expedition. On the day before his burial the captain and the first lieutenant were walking a short distance from the ship, pensively talking of the state of affairs and seeking an icy grave for their shipmate. What happened to them; and how all these plans were suddenly confounded as by an invisible hand, we must turn aside to explain.

CHAPTER XXIV.

THE DESERTED SHIPS.

IN the spring of 1852 England sent out the largest exploring fleet that had yet sailed. The names of the vessels will sound familiar to the reader. They were the "Assistance" and "Resolute," with their steamers, the "Pioneer" and "Intrepid," and the "North Star." The whole were under the command of Captain Edward Belcher. Captain Kellett had command of the "Resolute." The expedition sailed in April. In July it was pushing through the ice of Baffin Bay with a fleet of whalers. There was a lane of water into which the whalers and exploring fleet dropped, forming a long line, the American whaler, "M'Lellan," leading. The weather was fine, and all seemed going well. On the morning of the seventh word was passed from vessel to vessel that the "M'Lellan" had been caught in a nip and was sinking, her crew having already abandoned her. Hearing this, the sailors of the exploring fleet poured into her to take the sinking spoils. But Captain Belcher stopped that play, sent competent hands with powder, who blew up the ice which was crushing her, and set her free. But the next day she was nipped again, and this time the water poured into and soon sunk her to the water's edge. Belcher sent his men to save all that was possible out of her, and she was then blown up to get her out of the way of the other ships.

In August the squadron reached its headquarters at Beechey Island. The waters in every direction were remarkably free from ice. Captain Belcher with the "Assistance," towed by the "Pioneer," stood up Wellington Channel. Captain Kellett in the "Resolute," at the heels of the "Intrepid," pushed forward in an open sea toward Melville Island. The "North Star" remained at Beechey Island as a stationary store-ship to which escaping boat parties might flee.

We will follow Kellett's fortunes.

There was on board the "Investigator," which we have just left under M'Clure at Mercy Bay, a young man by the name of Creswell. His father's anxiety for his safety led him to wait upon the authorities in England just as Belcher was sailing and tender his advice. He told them that if the "Investigator" was beset in the ice west of Melville Island, as he thought she would be, then M'Clure would be sure to reach Melville Island by sledges and leave notice of his whereabouts. This was deemed good counsel, and now Kellett was following it under a full head of steam. We should have said that our old acquaintance, Lieutenant, now Captain M'Clintock, commanded the propeller "Intrepid," who, it will be remembered, had been at Melville Island with a sledge party the previous year, and examined Parry's records of thirty years before, and left additional ones of his own.

This energetic explorer soon, with the "Resolute" by the nose, after much thumping of the ice, put both vessels into the vicinity of Melville Island, and they went into winter-quarters at Dealy Island, on its south-eastern shore.

Now came the sledge-party excursions in every direction. A fine resolute young officer by the name of Mecham commanded that which was to trace the south line of Melville Island. He had two sledges, named the Discovery and the Fearless, a deposit of provisions which he was to carry forward for spring use and enough for twenty-five days' present use. Each sledge bore a little flag, given by home young ladies, with a sword arm on a white ground, and the motto, in Latin, "Over sea, land, and ice." Over frozen land, and through much ice and snow, the party sped. On their return, about the middle of October, Mecham turned aside to Parry's "Sandstone," and the cairn under which Parry and M'Clintock had already left records, and to which he was commanded to add one of his own. On opening it, and unrolling the parchments, he found M'Clure's deposit of April, 1852, about six months before! It contained M'Clure's voyaging and the discovery of the north-west passage, and his present position at Mercy Bay. It was the first news from his ship for two years, and such was the anxiety felt concerning him, that two vessels had been sent by way of Bering Strait to search for the searcher. Here was news of him not six months old! Here was news, too, of his great discovery not yet known to the world! Mecham built a new cairn, put into it his own record, and hurried off with his great news.

Captain Kellett was, of course, intensely desirous to send a party forward immediately to search for the "Investigator." But Mercy Bay was a hundred and seventy miles off, and the ice would be too weak for sledging, and too strong for boating until the darkness would prevent either. So they spent the winter as best they could. In March, while yet the peril of sledging was great, a party started, consisting of eleven men, under the command of Lieutenant Pim. This officer was in the "Herald," under Kellett, when she met M'Clure in the ice at Bering Strait. So he had been one of the last men who had said "good-bye" to the officers of the "Investigator."

He had now started with two sledges, the larger with seven men under his immediate command, and the smaller with two men under Dr. Domville.

Very slowly, and with great peril and toil, they made one hundred miles from the ship. Then the larger sledge, in slipping from a hummock, broke down. Here was a desperate state of the expedition! Domville advised a return with the smaller sledge. But Pim, after due deliberation, decided to take the dog-sledge and the two men, and push on, while Domville went into camp on the nearest land and waited his return, repairing in the mean time, if possible, the sledge.

On sped Pim with his dogs, which he fed with

preserved meat. One whole day he was sick and confined to the tent. They met with no game, yet onward they went. Weary days passed, and at last the Bay of Mercy was gained, but no "Investigator" could be seen. Straight across the bay went Pim, hoping to find a cairn and records. At two o'clock the men saw something black in the distance. Pim took his glass and looked. "Men, it's a ship!" he exclaimed, and all rushed forward. Pim soon got ahead, and saw two men walking slowly toward him. Pim ran and shouted and threw up his arms; as the wind and excitement prevented his words being heard, he was at first taken by the two men for one of their own party fleeing from a bear. As he came nearer, and they saw his face, black with the lamp smoke of his tent, and his violent gesticulation, they took him for an Esquimo, or a visitor from another world. Soon they heard, "I'm Lieutenant Pim, late of the 'Herald,' now in the 'Resolute.' Captain Kellett is in her at Dealy Island."

Pim was instantly in the presence of M'Clure and his lieutenant. Their hearts were too full for words, and the hardy navigators melted to tears. M'Clure says: "The announcement of relief being close at hand when none was supposed to be within the arctic circle was too sudden, unexpected, and joyous for our minds to comprehend it at once. The news flew with lightning rapidity; the ship was all in commotion; the sick, forgetful of their maladies, leaped from their hammocks; the artificers dropped their tools, and the lower deck was cleared of men, for they all rushed for the hatchway, to be assured that a stranger was actually among them, and that his tale was true. Despondency fled the ship, and Lieutenant Pim received a welcome, pure, hearty, and grateful, that he surely will remember and cherish to the end of his days."

Pim and his men, accompanied by M'Clure, returned in a few days. They found Dr. Domville and his party in good condition, having mended the sledge and killed five musk-oxen. All arrived safely at the harbor of the "Resolute" and "Intrepid."

For about two months communication was kept up between Dealy Island and Mercy Bay, and much consultation of the officers was held as to the course M'Clure should take. Captain Kellett at first favored M'Clure's plan of staying by the ship with a crew of the most hardy men. But a council of the surgeons pronounced the sanitary condition of the men as low and tending downward. Three arctic winters had made the robust puny. Only four among the healthy seamen came forward when asked to volunteer to stay, though the officers all voted to stand by the ship. In view of all these circumstances, it was decided to abandon the brave old "Investigator." Her boats, provisions, and equipments generally, were landed, and a well-guarded deposit was made of them for the use of Collinson, of the "Enterprise," who was supposed to be pushing for these waters; or for Franklin himself, should he or any of his expedition be alive and drifting toward Mercy Bay. On the third of June, 1853, the colors were thrown to the breeze, and officers and crew bade farewell to the "Investigator."

It seemed an ignominious ending of her noble career to be left alone in the darkness, cold, and dreariness of this arctic region, to hear no sounds of life except those of the croaking raven, the howling wolf, and the barking fox. But we presume her retiring men, glad to save their own lives by a wonderful deliverance, indulged in no sickly sentiment over the vessel.

In a few weeks the sixty men of the "Investigator" were comfortably settled on board the "Resolute" and "Intrepid," in the midst of abundance and good companionship. Lieutenant Creswell, whose father had prompted the plan which had saved the expedition in which he sailed, was sent to Beechey Island with dispatches for the home authorities. When he arrived at the island the "Phœnix" had just arrived with supplies for Belcher, having left home in the spring. In her he sailed to England, where he arrived in October, and was cordially greeted. He had not only seen the north-west passage but had gone through it.

Kellett, having by sledge parties searched in vain, far and near, for traces of Franklin, made arrangements to take his ships to Beechey Island. It was now midsummer, and the ice might break up at any time. He built a storehouse on the island, and having filled it with provisions left in it this record;—

"This is a house which I have named the Sailor's Home, under the especial patronage of my Lords Commissioners of the Admiralty. *Here* royal sailors and mariners are fed, clothed, and receive double pay for inhabiting it."

The ice did not let the vessels go until the middle of August. They sailed twenty-four hours and then it held them fast again. The days of summer wore away and winter approached, and still no open sea, nor even leads through which they might bore, appeared. Game was plenty, musk-oxen especially; of this highly fragrant beef they obtained and froze ten thousand pounds. In September a gale piled the ice-pack about them, made an island of their ice encasement, and set them drifting whither they would not. Having toyed with them two whole months, they were let alone for the winter in a good position due east from Winter Harbor, and in longitude 101° west. Here, in tolerable comfort, the spring of 1854 found them, one only having died.

In the early part of the spring M'Clure went with his men, on sledges, to Beechey Island and took possession of the store-ship. Soon after an order came from Belcher commanding Kellett to abandon his ships and come to Beechey Island. Kellett remonstrated, saying that his position was a good one for an early escape; that he had a plenty of supplies; that the expedition was in good health, and that parties concerned in deserting ships under such circumstances "would deserve to have the jackets taken off their backs."

Belcher seems to have considered this strong talk for a subordinate, and he sent a peremptory order to abandon the ships. Two of Kellett's sledge parties were out on distant surveys. Leaving orders for their guidance, he prepared his vessels for abandonment. The engines of the "Intrepid" were so left that the ship could be got under steam in two hours. Both vessels were well provisioned, and made ready, in every respect, for occupation. He then calked down the hatches, all hands took their last look of the "Resolute" and "Intrepid," and started on their sledge journey. They arrived at Beechey Island safely, utterly surprising M'Clure and his men.

During all of the time in which we have been following the expedition of Kellett, Captain Belcher was surveying Wellington Channel and its adjacent waters. He had wintered in the ice, and extended his search, fall and spring, by sledge parties. In August of this year, 1854, his ships, the "Assistance" and "Pioneer," were liberated. He immediately pushed for Beechey Island. Waters about this island were at the same time navigable, and the leads extended fifteen miles up the channel. There was a belt of ice only twenty miles wide between his ships and this open highway homeward, and this belt was much cracked. Yet Captain Belcher was intent on hurrying home, with seeming impatience of all arctic restraints. He abandoned his ships on the twenty-sixth of August, and all hands made their way to Beechey Island. The sledge- parties came in, one after another. The spirited Mecham had extended his survey across the track of the "Enterprise," commanded by Captain Collinson, the consort, it will be recollected, of the "Investigator." He was, in 1852, not far in the rear of M'Clure.

The sledges being all in, the officers and crews of the five ships, the "Investigator," "Resolute," "Intrepid," "Assistance," and "Pioneer," were put on board the "North Star," and the sails were spread for home. Just then the "Phœnix," returned from her home trip with Lieutenant Creswell, accompanied by the "Talbot," both under Captain Inglefield, hove in sight, rounding Cape Riley. The men were then distributed in the three ships. On the twenty-eighth of September they landed safely in England.

A breeze, of course, was raised by Belcher's extraordinary feat of leaving four of his five ships behind him. He was court-martialed, acquitted, and *knighted.* M'Clure received the knighting without the court-martialing, and upon him and his officers and men were bestowed the fifty thousand dollars offered by the Government for the discovery of the north-west passage. M'Clure's superior officer, Collinson, brought his ship, the "Enterprise," back through the waters he had entered. Nothing had been added to the hints which had been found by Austin at Beechey Island, in the early searching, to the knowledge of Franklin's fate. The well-guarded dominions of ice and cold still held their sad secret.

Some of our readers will recollect the remarkable later history of the veteran "Resolute," one of these abandoned ships. We can but glance at it. In 1855 Captain Buddington, of New London, Conn., in the whale-ship "George Henry," found the "Resolute," imbedded in an ice-raft, drifting through Baffin Bay. She had already made twelve hundred miles of her homeward trip. There was some ice in her hold; mold and damp had damaged some things, but otherwise she was essentially as Kellett had left her. Good fires in her stoves removed the dampness and melted the ice, and her fine force-pumps removed the water. Her rigging was repaired, and some new sails set. In a few days she freed herself from the ice, and Captain Buddington, with ten picked men from the "George Henry," arrived safely with her in New London the twenty-fourth of December after a rough passage of over two months. The English authorities relinquished all claims upon her. Congress then purchased her of the owners of the "George Henry," and she was put into the naval dock at Brooklyn and thoroughly repaired. Every article left in her by Kellett was restored. She was then manned by a naval crew and put in command of Captain Hartstein, and, "with sails all set and streamers all afloat," she bore away for her English home. When she reached British waters she was honored as a veteran covered with scars returning from many victorious battle-fields. The highest naval officers hastened on board of her. The queen herself paid her a visit. Complimentary ensigns fluttered from every flag-staff.

Cannon thundered their noisy welcome in every direction. The pulse of the whole nation beat with joy. The queen sent a distinguished artist to put the "reception" on canvas for the royal gallery.

The American officers who brought her home were made the nation's guest, with such hospitality as few if any strangers ever received. The seamen under them had substantial remembrance from the queen's private purse. Old England and the younger England of America met for once with hearty congratulations.

The "Resolute" herself retired on her laurels, it is presumed, henceforth, if not knighted and pensioned, yet exempt from further labor and peril.

CHAPTER XXV.

THE FATE OF SIR JOHN FRANKLIN.

SHORTLY after the return of Belcher and M'Clure a new sensation was given to the interest attending the fate of Sir John Franklin.

Dr. Rae, a veteran explorer in the employment oft he Hudson Bay Company, published a letter in the Montreal "Herald" of October 21, 1854, directed to the governor of that company. Its substance was as follows:—

In the spring of 1853 the doctor started down the Back, or Great Fish River. On reaching its mouth he went east and north, being directed to extend the survey of the western shore of Boothia, a region toward which we have sailed with Parry when on his second voyage. Here he met with Esquimo who seemed intelligent above the average of their countrymen. In the possession of these natives were various articles at once recognized as belonging to the lost explorers! Here there was a clew to the secret which had caused many hearts to ache, to reveal which two great nations had long been devoting large treasures, and the services of their best men. Rae, of course, bent all his energies to the following up of the clew thus given. Falling in with Esquimo hunters from time to time, he ascertained that nearly all of them had heard of the party of white men from whom these articles had been obtained. The amount of the information obtained by comparing these statements was in substance this:—

In the spring, four winters ago, (1850,) several Esquimo families were hunting seal on the north shore of a large island. The island was many days' journey to the west and beyond a great river. Dr. Rae at once understood this to be what was known as King William's Land. While these Esquimo were thus employed they saw forty white men traveling to the south over the ice, along the west shore of the island. They were dragging a boat and sledges. They looked very thin, were getting short of provisions, and were going south where they could shoot deer. They could not talk in the Esquimo language, but they contrived to purchase some seals of the natives, and to make known the fact that their ship or ships had been crushed by the ice. Later in the season, but before the breaking up of the ice, the dead bodies of thirty persons and some graves were seen on the main land, and other bodies on an island near it. These bodies were a day's journey from the mouth of a great river, (Great Fish River,) and to the north-west of it. Some of the bodies were in a tent or tents. Some were under a boat which had been turned up to shelter them. One of the men had a telescope strapped over his shoulder, and his double-barreled gun lay underneath him. It was no doubt that of an officer. Sad evidence was given from the mutilated state of some of the bodies, and the contents of the kettles, that the wretched survivors had been driven to the desperate resort of feeding upon the flesh of their fellow-comrades. Some had survived until the sea-fowl began to return, maybe till the end of May, for shots were heard, and feathers and fresh bones of birds were found near some of the bodies.

Rae purchased as many mementos of the sad facts as he could bring away; they were at the same time assurances of the truth of the tales which had been told him. Among these were parts of watches, telescopes, compasses, and guns, all of which had evidently been broken up by the ignorant natives. Silver spoons, silver table-forks, and other table plate were obtained. Some of these were engraved with Franklin's name; others with the names of his officers. In some cases the names of the ships, "Erebus" or "Terror," were added.

Dr. Rae immediately hastened to England. The fate of Sir John Franklin and his entire expedition was regarded as decided, and Dr. Rae and his men received the offered reward of fifty thousand dollars as the first discoverers of the sad fact.

The English Government considered it morally impossible that any one of the expedition should be alive, and declined to peril the lives of other brave men by encouraging further search. But Lady Franklin devoted all her available remaining fortune for one more search to be directed to the very region named by the Esquimo. Others came forward to aid in the expense. A steam-propeller yacht of one hundred and seventy tons was purchased, named the "Fox"—a small craft, indeed, to go unattended on such an errand. But love gave the vessel wings and courage. She was commanded by our good friend, Captain M'Clintock. The under officers and crew were picked men. Carl Petersen, whom we have met in Sir John Ross' last expedition, a tried man and apt interpreter of Esquimo talk, was secured from Denmark, his native land. The yacht was well stocked with provisions and scientific instruments.

The "Fox," having reached the Greenland coast, touched at a Danish settlement, where additional coal, furs, and some other articles for an arctic winter were obtained. Dogs and dog-sledges were also added to their outfit. An Esquimo dog-driver, by the name of Christian, volunteered his services, was taken on board, was washed, cropped, and dressed in sailor clothes, after which he strutted about among the men with great satisfaction. There was a hand-organ on board, with which he was greatly delighted. He proved very useful in the management of the dogs, and in teaching that art to the officers.

These dogs exhibited the characteristics of their race, sometimes to the amusement, but often to the sore vexation, of their managers. There was one of the pack named Harness Jack. Sledge-dogs are said to eat every thing except fox and raven, but Harness Jack gobbled down a raven with a gusto. He had a notion to wear his harness continually. If when he had been off in the sledge an attempt was made to take it off, he showed his teeth most decidedly.

Jack was a favorite among the sailors and a tyrant among his kind. There came one day to another dog a whole family of little ones. Her kennel was an empty barrel laid on its side for that purpose. Harness Jack mounted the barrel, and though most uncomfortably situated, stood watch over the helpless brood night and day. But for him the mother would have been bereft of her children, for Esquimo dogs have the amiable propensity of eating young puppies. It is not at all certain that if Jack had not been well fed for his disinterested service, he would not himself have indulged in the luxury of tender young dogs for breakfast. We hope we do not wrong him by the thought.

On one occasion an officer attempted to kick Jack for his too great familiarity, and accidentally sent his seal-skin slipper from his foot after him. Jack picked up the slipper, scampered away to a hiding-place, and gulped it down his throat in a twinkling.

The "Fox," of course, tried the terrible passage of Melville Bay, to reach the western shore through the north water. The distance across this bay is one hundred and seventy miles. They had made one hundred and twenty of it in the early part of September, 1857. A few days later a terrific gale came on and broke up the floe. From this time our little craft was made a plaything by the winds and currents, they sending it whither they pleased, only being seldom pleased to carry it in the direction its captain desired to go. It was the old game played with De Haven and others. The "Fox" did not get rid of the ice by which it was firmly held until late in April, 1858! During this unwilling voyaging it drifted out of Melville into Baffin Bay, and southward through Davis Strait, and out into the Atlantic Ocean, a distance of thirteen hundred and eighty-five miles!

The winter which was thus spent in the villainous pack was attended by many perils but no serious incident. The sailors contrived to get some merriment out of Guy Fawkes' day, and much healthful amusement, and as well as substantial profit, out of seal and bear shooting.

Nothing daunted by this worse than loss of one entire year, Captain M'Clintock turned about and tried again. This time he succeeded, and on the sixteenth of July was in Lancaster Sound. He steamed into Barrow Strait to the old station at Beechey Island. From this he continued west, and then south, into what may be found on the map as Peel Sound, between North Somerset and Prince of Wales' Island. Keeping near the coast, he attempted to push through this long, narrow, and continually narrowing sound as he went south, which opens into a broader water which washes the shores on which Dr. Rae's Esquimo had seen the wrecked white men. But twenty-five miles was all the southing the ice would allow him to make.

Going back into Barrow Strait, the "Fox" steamed down Prince Regent Inlet on the east side of North Somerset. On the extreme south of this land is a strait, twenty miles long and one wide, called Bellot Strait. M'Clintock had been on this strait nine years before when with Captain James Ross, but it was yet but little known. Captain M'Clintock hoped with trembling to sail through it into the southern part of Peel Sound, and so get round the solid ice which had stopped him on the west side of North Somerset. He did push into it, and made half the passage through. He then fell into the grip of the pack and was drifted back entirely out of it. Again he went in, and again was driven out. Five times did the persevering "Fox" push its pugnacious nose into Bellot Strait, and the fifth time it pushed through! They found a snug creek which they named Port Kennedy, and went into winter-quarters.

Bellot Strait divides North Somerset from a broad land called Boothia Felix. South-east of Boothia and about one hundred and fifty miles from M'Clintock's present wintering-place is King William Island. This last was the island where Rae's Esquimo obtained their Sir John Franklin relics. Opposite the winter harbor, Port Kennedy, is the southern shore of Prince of Wales Island.

No sooner were the winter comforts secured, than the wide-awake M'Clintock began to prepare for sledging in the spring on a large scale. Three parties, with dog-sledges, each of four men, were to be sent out. The first, under the captain himself, accompanied by Petersen the interpreter, was to examine the shores of King William Island, and push forward to the mouth of the Great Fish River. The second, under Lieutenant Hobson, was to survey the west coast of Boothia. The third, under officer Young, was to strike across the sound to Prince of Wales Island, and follow its shore along its southern, and a considerable distance up its western, line.

The winter passed away with its full share of arctic comforts and pleasures. The captain thought that the greatest addition to pleasures which could well be conceived would be a well-filled letter-bag! One sad event occurred. The engineer died suddenly of apoplexy. There was no one in the vessel competent to take his place.

The sledge parties were off at the early day of March 3, 1859, while yet winter, and ice, and storms ruled the days. The captain soon fell in with the natives, many of whom had relics of the lost "Erebus" and "Terror." They had not seen either the ships or the wrecked men from whom they came, but the account they gave of both agreed perfectly with the stories told Dr. Rae.

Having obtained this information, M'Clintock returned to the "Fox." The other parties had come in. These were only preparatory trips. The three great journeys commenced the second of April.

M'Clintock and Hobson traveled together until they came over against Cape Felix, the north point of King William Island. The natives spoke of the ships being wrecked on the west side of this island, one sinking and the other drifting ashore, the latter being the source of the relics they possessed. The men, they said, went away toward the Great River, and the next year their bones were found scattered along the way.

Hobson hastened on to the alleged locality of the wreck. The captain examined the east shore of this great island, and then went over to the mainland and made diligent search about the mouth of the Great Fish River. Returning, he led his party up the western shore of King William Island, along the very track which Franklin's retreating men must have passed. The sledges kept on the ice, and some of the party walked on the shore, carefully examining every trace. While Captain M'Clintock was walking on a gravel ridge, which the winds kept in a measure bare of snow, he came upon a human skeleton. It was partly exposed, with a few fragments of clothes lying near. The perfectly bleached skeleton was lying upon its face. The limbs and smaller bones were either dissevered, or gnawed away by small animals. A careful examination of the ground was made, and more pieces of clothing, a pocket-book, a clothes-brush, pocket-comb, a neck-handkerchief with a loose bow-knot, a blue jacket, and a pilot cloth great-coat with plain-covered buttons. All these articles, with the style of dress, showed that the deceased was a steward's or officer's servant. He had taken the gravel ridge for easier travel, fallen on his face and died. It reminded the captain of the remark of an old Esquimo woman who had seen the escaping party: "They fell down and died as they walked away."

Going on a little farther, M'Clintock found a cairn put up by Lieutenant Hobson. He had been as far south as this spot, and returned north only six days before. He had left a note for M'Clintock which gave important information. He had not found the wreck nor seen any natives, but he had found a record left by Franklin's party. This lifted in part the vail which had hid the secret of their fate for so many years. Hobson had found it at Point Victory, on the north-west coast of this island—King William Island. The record paper was a printed form supplied to all the arctic ships, and was soldered up in a thin tin cylinder. The writing was upon the margin and read as follows:—

"Twenty-eighth of May, 1847.—H. M. ships 'Erebus' and 'Terror' wintered in the ice in lat. 70° 5′ N., long. 98° 23′ W.

"Having wintered in 1845-6 at Beechey Island in lat. 74° 43′ 28″ N., long. 91° 39′ 15″ W., after having ascended Wellington Channel to lat. 77° and returned by the west side of Cornwallis Island.

"Sir John Franklin commanding the expedition.

"All well.

"Party consisting of two officers and six men left the ships on Monday, twenty-fourth of May, 1847. "G. M. GORE, *Lieutenant.*

"CHARLES F. DES VŒUX, *Mate.*"

Thus far Franklin's expedition was one of almost unexampled success. From the time they were last seen, by the whaler, in Baffin Bay, July 1843, they had made the passage of Lancaster Sound and Barrow Strait, had pushed up Wellington Channel a hundred and fifty miles to the highest latitude ever attained, returned through an unexplored channel west of Cornwallis Island, and wintered at Beechey Island. Then they had sailed south to their present position, and spent, in comfort and health, a second winter. They had sailed through five hundred miles of previously unexplored waters. They were now within ninety miles of the known waters leading out through Bering Strait to the Atlantic and dear old England! The north-west passage must have appeared to Franklin as almost certainly known to him, and to be easily demonstrated by a boat journey, if not by his ships themselves. But how soon was all changed! The record we have just noticed, written by officer Gore in May, 1847, was taken out in April, 1848, and, by another hand, the following addition made on the margin:—

"*April* 25, 1848.—H. M. ships 'Terror' and Erebus' were deserted on the twenty-second of April, five leagues N. N. W. of this, having been beset since the twelfth of September, 1846. The officers and crews, one hundred and five souls, under the command of Captain F. R. M. Crozier, landed here in lat. 69° 37′ 42″ N., and long. 98° 41′ W. Sir John Franklin died on the eleventh of June, 1847; and the total loss by death in the expedition has been to this date nine officers and fifteen men.

(Signed) F. R. M. CROZIER,
Captain and Senior Officer.

(Signed) JAMES FITZJAMES,
Captain H. M. S. Erebus,

and start (on) to-morrow, 26, for Back's Fish River."

A small additional note on the margin states the fact that the document had been removed to its present place of deposit, four miles, from the place where "the *late* Commander Gore had put it."

Gore himself then was dead, and only two weeks after he had written "All well," his noble commander, Franklin, ended his eminent life.

Captain M'Clintock now made the best speed possible on the track of Hobson. After passing the extreme west point of King William Land, which they named Cape Crozier, they came upon a boat. This Hobson had seen, and left a note stating the fact.

This boat, its contents and surroundings, constituted the saddest relic yet seen. Large quantities of damaged clothing was scattered about in it, but no record, pocket-book, memorandum, nor journal of any kind, was found; no name, even, was found on any article of clothing. The boat was swept and examined in every crevice.

The boat was of light but strong material, and rested upon a stout-built sledge. It had been evidently equipped in every particular for the desperate expedition up the Great Fish River.

The most impressive relic of the boat was two skeletons: one of a young man, the other that of a strongly made man of middle age. They were much broken, and the skulls were entirely missing. Wolves had evidently visited the boat. Near them were two double-barreled guns and five watches. A large quantity of silverware, with names of owners engraved on them, with a great variety of such valuables, were found. The Esquimo had not been here.

No graves nor other skeletons were found in the vicinity. The boat's bow was directed toward the ships, back to which her men were evidently dragging her. This may account for only two skeletons, and the small quantity of food found—a little tea, forty pounds of chocolate, and a small quantity of pemmican. The rest of them may have gone forward to the ships, sixty-five miles, intending to return.

M'Clintock, after the most complete search, which did not add any material item to his information, returned to his ship. The sledge excursions were all ended late in July. Young had made valuable discoveries, but had seen no traces of Franklin. Both Young and Hobson were much broken in health, and the commander was admonished if he would save his men and vessel he must improve the earliest opportunity of getting away. On the third of August they moved a few miles; on the tenth they got up steam, the captain, by the aid of the firemen, contriving to manage the engine, and made good headway; on the twenty-eighth they were at a Danish port in Greenland, and on the twenty-first of September Captain M'Clintock was in London.

Honor and reward awaited the officers and crew of the brave little "Fox." The relics were deposited in the United Service Institution. The fate of Franklin and his men was discovered. If money, bravery, and good-will could have saved them, our last chapter would have read, Franklin saved!

THE END.

Lindsay Lee and his Friends.

A Story for the Time. Large 16mo............ $0 75

Gustavus Adolphus,

The Hero of the Reformation. From the French of L Abelous. By Mrs. C. A. LACROIX. Illustrated. Large 16mo............................ 1 00

Heroine of the White Nile;

Or, What a Woman Did and Dared. A Sketch of the Remarkable Travels and Experiences of Miss Alexandrine Tinné. By Prof. WILLIAM WELLS. Illustrated. Large 16mo............. 1 00

Memoir of Washington Irving.

With Selections from his Works, and Criticisms. By CHARLES ADAMS, D.D. Large 16mo........ 1 25

Itinerant Side;

Or, Pictures of Life in the Itinerancy. With Engravings.................................... 1 00

Life of Dr. Samuel Johnson.

By C. ADAMS, D.D. Large 16mo............... 1 50

Lady Huntingdon Portrayed.

Including Brief Sketches of some of her Friends and Colaborers. By the Author of "The Missionary Teacher," "Sketches of Mission Life," etc. 1 25

Ministering Children.

A Story showing how even a Child may be as a Ministering Angel of Love to the Poor and Sorrowful. Illustrated...... .... 1 50

Lives made Sublime by Faith and Works.

Large 16mo. Illustrated..................... 1 25

My Sister Margaret.

A Temperance Story. Four Illustrations. By Mrs. C. M. EDWARDS............. .... 1 25

Palissy the Potter;

Or, the Huguenot, Artist, and Martyr. A True Narrative. By C. L. BRIGHTWELL. Illustrated. 1 25

Footprints of Roger Williams.

By Rev. Z. A. MUDGE. Large 16mo........... $1 25

Path of Life.

By D. WISE, D.D. Large 16mo............... 1 00
Gilt Edge.................................. 1 30

The Ministry of Life.

By MARIA LOUISA CHARLESWORTH, Author of "Ministering Children," etc. With Illustrations 1 25

Pleasant Pathways;

Or, Persuasives to Early Piety. By DANIEL WISE, D.D. Steel Engravings................ 1 25

The Poet Preacher:

A Brief Memorial of Charles Wesley, the Eminent Preacher and Poet. By CHARLES ADAMS. Illustrated....................................... 1 00

The Stony Road.

A Scottish Story from Real Life. Large 16mo.. 0 85

Pillars of Truth.

A Series of Sermons on the Decalogue. By E. O HAVEN, D.D.............................. 1 25

The Rainbow Side.

A Sequel to "The Itinerant." By Mrs. C. M. EDWARDS. With Four Illustrations........... 1 25

The Shepherd King;

Or, a Sick Minister's Lectures on the Shepherd of Bethlehem, and the Blessing that followed Them. By A. L. O. E., Authoress of the "Young Pilgrim," "The Roby Family," etc. Illustrated. 1 25

Trials of an Inventor:

Life and Discoveries of Charles Goodyear. Large 16mo.. 1 25

Views from Plymouth Rock.

By Z. A. MUDGE. With Six Illustrations. Large 16mo.................................... 1 50

Words that Shook the World;

Or, Martin Luther his own Biographer. Being Pictures of the Great Reformer, sketched mainly from his own Sayings. By CHARLES ADAMS. Illustrated $1 25

Young Lady's Counselor.

By D. WISE, D.D. Large 16mo 1 00
Gilt Edge.................................. 1 30

Young Man's Counselor.

By D. WISE, D.D. Large 16mo 1 00
Gilt Edge.................................. 1 30

Six Years in India.

By MR. HUMPHREYS.............................. 1 25

Young Shetlander and his Home.

Being a Biographical Sketch of Young Thomas Edmonston, the Naturalist, and an Interesting Account of the Shetland Islands. By B. K. PEIRCE, D.D. Illustrated. Large 16mo....... 1 25

Children of Lake Huron;

Or, the Cousins at Cloverley. 16mo............ 1 25

Dora Hamilton;

Or, Sunshine and Shadow. Six Illustrations. 16mo.. 0 90

Discipline of Alice Lee.

A Truthful Temperance Story. Illustrated. 16mo.. 1 00

Suzanna De L'Orme.

A Story of Huguenot Times. Large 16mo.. 1 25

The Christian Statesman.

A Portraiture of Sir Thomas Fowell Buxton. By Z. A. MUDGE.................................. 1 25

The Forest Boy.

A Sketch of the Life of Abraham Lincoln. By Z. A. MUDGE. Large 16mo 1 25

Afternoons with Grandma.

From the French of Madame Carraud. By Mrs. Mary Kinmont. Beautifully Illustrated. Bound in Muslin. 16mo..$1 25

Household Stories.

From the German of Madame Ottilie Wildermuth. By Miss Eleanor Kinmont. With Illustrations. 16mo. Four Volumes. Each.............................. 1 25

Father's Coming Home.

By the Author of "Weldon Woods." Four Illustrations. 16mo.. 1 00

Agnes Morton's Trial;

Or, the Lost Diamonds. And **The Young Governess.** By Mrs. Emma N. Janvier. 12mo.................. 1 25

My Sister Margaret.

A Temperance Story. By Mrs. C. M. Edwards. Illustrated. 12mo.................................... 1 25

Lilian.

A Story of the Days of Martyrdom in England Three Hundred Years Ago. Five Illustrations. 16mo...... 90

Ethel Linton;

Or, The Feversham Temper. By E. A. W., Author of "The Home of the Davenports," etc. 12mo.......... 1 25

Simple Stories with Odd Pictures;

Or, Evening Amusements for the Little Ones at Home. With Twenty Illustrations by Paul Konewka. 16mo. 75

Young Life;

Or, The Boys and Girls of Pleasant Valley. By Mrs. Sarah A. Mather, Author of "Itinerant Side," etc. 12mo.. 1 25

Fraulein Mina;

Or, Life in an American German Family. By Miss Mary H. Norris. 12mo............................ 1 25

Through Trials to Triumph.

A Story of Boy's School-life. By Miss H. A. Putnam. Illustrated. 12mo................................ 1 25

Glaucia.
A Story of Athens in the First Century. By Emma Leslie. Illustrated. 12mo $1 25

Talks with Girls.
By Augusta Larned. 12mo 1 50

Peter, the Apprentice.
An Historical Tale of the Reformation in England. By the author of "Faithful, but not Famous," etc. 16mo. 90

Romance without Fiction.
Or, Sketches from the Portfolio of an Old Missionary. By Rev. Henry Bleby. 12mo 1 75

The Man of One Book;
Or, the Life of the Rev. William Marsh, D.D. By his Daughter. Edited by Daniel Wise. 12mo 1 50

Sunday Afternoons.
A Book for Little People. By E. F. Burr, D.D., author of "Ecce-Celum." 16mo 75

Little Princess,
And other Stories, chiefly about Christmas. By Aunt Hattie. 18mo 65

School-Life of Ben and Bentie.
Illustrated. 18mo 90

Peeps at our Sunday-Schools.
By Rev. Alfred Taylor. 12mo 1 25

Elizabeth Tudor:
The Queen and the Woman. By Virginia F. Townsend. Illustrated. 12mo 1 50

True Stories of the American Fathers.
For the Girls and Boys all over the Land. By Miss Rebecca M'Conkey. Illustrated. 12mo 1 50

Glimpses of our Lake Region in 1863,
And other Papers. By Mrs. H. C. Gardner. 12mo... 1 50

Through the Eye to the Heart;
Or, Eye-Teaching in the Sunday-School. By Rev. W. F. Crafts. 12mo 1 50

Discontent,
And other Stories. By Mrs. H. C. Gardner. 12mo... 1 25

www.ingramcontent.com/pod-product-compliance
Lightning Source LLC
LaVergne TN
LVHW020231110826
845151LV00003B/894

* 9 7 8 1 4 2 5 5 3 0 7 2 3 *